I0479019

The Authority of
Divided Authority Federalism

Alan Scott Hammurabi

RoseDog Books
PITTSBURGH, PENNSYLVANIA 15238

The contents of this work including, but not limited to, the accuracy of events, people, and places depicted; opinions expressed; permission to use previously published materials included; and any advice given or actions advocated are solely the responsibility of the author, who assumes all liability for said work and indemnifies the publisher against any claims stemming from publication of the work.

All Rights Reserved
Copyright © 2018 by Alan Scott Hammurabi

No part of this book may be reproduced or transmitted, downloaded, distributed, reverse engineered, or stored in or introduced into any information storage and retrieval system, in any form or by any means, including photocopying and recording, whether electronic or mechanical, now known or hereinafter invented without permission in writing from the author.

RoseDog Books
585 Alpha Drive
Suite 103
Pittsburgh, PA 15238
Visit our website at www.rosedogbookstore.com

ISBN: 978-1-4809-8128-7
eISBN: 978-1-4809-8105-8

TABLE OF CONTENTS

No Political truth is certainly of greater intrinsic value or is stamped with the authority of more enlightened patrons of liberty than that on which the objection is founded. *The accumulation of all powers legislative, executive and judiciary in the same hands, whether of one, a few or many, and whether hereditary, self appointed, or elective, may justly be the definition of tyranny.* Were the federal constitution therefore really chargeable with this accumulation of power or with a *mixture of powers having a dangerous tendency to such an accumulation,* no further arguments would be necessary to inspire a universal reprobation of the system. I persuade myself however, that it will be made apparent to every one, that *the charge cannot be supported,* and that the maxim on which it relies, has been totally misconceived and misapplied. *In order to form correct ideas on this important subject, it will be proper to investigate the sense, in which the preservation of liberty requires, that the three great departments of power should be separate and distinct.*

-The Federalist no. 47

INTRODUCTION

I hold these truths to be self-evident: one cannot know what ought to be without knowing what is, not what is without knowing what was, and not what was without the intellectual origins.

Federalism and the Early American Republic have been misunderstood by the masses for some time. To be sure, federalism is inherently a very complex concept. The concepts importance though may be the essence of its importance in terms of governance history. Federalism is the result of social tumult and polity decay. It is a call for order. It is a natural formulation in times of crisis to answer the call for order. Federalism may be the most important discovery of the Early American Republic; one that had generations of experience with tyranny, anarchy, despotism, and unwarranted consolidations of power with no remedy. Federalism was an intellectual endeavor that formulated out of natural order and ingenuity to stabilize a polity.

This book argues three points: 1) There was a revolution in the mode of thought of the people, but most importantly the intellectual elite whom established the American government and laws. 2) That federalism has a natural formulation and clear, yet complex, definition. The epicenter of which is premised on division. And 3) The framers of the General Convention of 1787 used their vast intellect, experience, and reason to foster divided authority federalism into the U.S. Constitution. The concluding remarks are a generous, humble, yet ambitious attempt to bring scholars together across disciplines to discover and prove that federalism is a law of nature and needs to be adhered to in conjunction with using the law of nature on a global scale.

CHAPTER I —

Mode of Thought in the Early American Republic

> What do we mean by the Revolution? The war?
> That was no part of the Revolution; it was only an
> effect and consequence of it. The Revolution was in
> the minds of the people, and this was effected, from
> 1760 to 1775, fifteen years before a drop of blood
> was shed at Lexington.
>
> —John Adams to Thomas Jefferson, 1815

The Dichotomy of Literature, Sources, and Modes of Thought
True revolutionary eras commence not with the sword, but with the mind. Whereas it is true that the sword must, in most circumstances, be a sufficient conditional to this end, it does not follow that the sword is the necessary conditional. Traditions, laws, rules, and doctrines since time immemorable end with the concept ending within the mind of mankind. None more so is this the case than in the Early American Republic.

The Early American Republic underwent revolutionary changes in the mode of thought of colonials of all statuses, with respect to governance (structure, civil discourse, pragmatic execution) and law. The number of penned pamphlets on theory, English statutory and common law, liberty, and governance were of prodigious note.[1] Every medium was open and to many if they so choose to write. The penned pieces of the time of the American Revolution were heated and paradigm altering attacks on the common English order.[2] More-

---

[1] Bernard Bailyn, *The Ideological Origins of the American Revolution* (Cambridge, Massachusetts: The Belknap Press of Harvard University Press, 1967), 1-21.

[2] The Introduction to Thomas Paine's Common Sense (1776) states: PERHAPS the

over, rebuttals to extravagant and revolutionary polemicists, from the colonial perspective, were just as wide spread.[3] This surely extended all throughout the era until, at least, 1789. This reality of the Early American Republic, inter alia, has caused some scholars to denote this era as The Age of Passion and some The Age of Enlightenment.[4] Notwithstanding the various denotations, it is beyond reasonable doubt that the revolution that mattered the most was within the minds of colonial Americans of all statuses. One great challenge is to sift through the statuses and rhetoric of the time, discern what prompted the changes, and to what end with respect to the common people and the intellectual elite of the Early American Republic. The next is to understand the changes in the mode of thought of those that actually contributed in the creation thereof (the intellectual elite of the time).

There is a dichotomy at this juncture: the loud writers (the common, hysterical polemicists) and the meaningful writers (the intellectual elite of the time). The former outweighs the latter in volume and spirit, but the latter surpasses the former in quality and everlasting wisdom. The former oscillated the minds of the common people, no less historically significant, but the latter is where the conceptual changes manifested into governance and law. Of the particular revolutionary changes actuated, those of governance and law, this came from a particular class status: the

---

sentiments contained in the following pages, are not yet sufficiently fashionable to procure them general favor; a long habit of not thinking a thing wrong, gives it superficial appearance of being right, and raises at first formidable outcry in defence of custom. But the tumult soon subsides. Times make more converts than reason. Also see: Pauline Maier, "A Pearl in a Gnarled Shell: Gordon S. Wood's The Creation of the American Republic Reconsidered," The William and Mary Quarterly Vol. 44, No. 3 (1987): 585. "The 'great intellectual force of Common Sense' therefore lay, as Bernard Bailyn observed, in 'its reversal of the presumptions' that had shaped previous political argumentation. Paine challenged the 'basic constitutional paradigm' of his time."

[3] Bailyn, *The Ideological Origins of the American Revolution*, 5. "Any number of people could join in such proliferating polemics, and rebuttals could come from all sides. Thomas Paine's Common Sense was answered not merely by two exhaustive refutations by Tories but also by at least four pamphlets written by patriots who shared his desire for independence but not his constitutional and religious views or his assumptions about human nature."

[4] Marshall Smelser, "The Federalist Period as an Age of Passion," *American Quarterly* Vol. 10, No. 4 (1958). For an instantiation of this concept into the American Revolution era see: Elkins and McKitrick, *The Age of Federalism* (New York & Oxford: Oxford University Press, 1993), 4-5.

intellectual elites. This dichotomy, in its simplest form, is best shown in the minds and relationship of Thomas Paine and John Adams. The common versus the intellectual elite.

The significance of Paine's *Common Sense* has not been under recognized in the historical literature. In fact, it may be over recognized by scholars of old and more contemporary times that have wrote in respect to the history of our governance and law. Notwithstanding, some such as Bernard Bailyn, takes a more objective approach to understanding Paine. Bailyn highlights the significance of Paine's *Common Sense*, but then retracts such in that it had "two exhaustive refutations."[5] These refutations, or counter arguments, were by the intellectual elite (most notably Adams). Whereas, more recent scholarship has suggested that if one wants to pen on the Early American Republic, Paine's importance must be noted, as Pauline Maier criticizes Gordon Wood for. Wood argues that the American Revolution was in the name of the English constitution as opposed to being a direct refutation thereof.[6] Pauline Maier respectfully charges that Wood failed to acknowledge the significance of Paine and that "Wood could claim, moreover, that the colonists revolted on behalf of the English constitution only by denying the importance traditionally and correctly attributed to Paine's sweeping attack on that constitution."[7] With great respect, Paine did not garnish nearly the support attributed to his works by the intellectual elite (the ones that manifested change). As Charles Inglis, a repeatable loyalist, pens:

> I find no COMMON SENSE in this pamphlet, but much UNCOMMON phrenzy. It is an outrageous insult on the common sense of Americans; an insidious attempt to poison their minds, and seduce them from their loyalty and truest interest. The principles

---

[5] Bailyn, *The Ideological Origins of the American Revolution*, 5.

[6] Gordon Wood, *The Creation of the American Republic 1776-1787* (University of North Carolina Press, 1969).

[7] Maier, "A Pearl in a Gnarled Shell," 585. Additionally, it is implicit within this section a defense of Wood negating Paine for the complex analysis of the history of our Constitution. This should not be construed in any other way.

of government laid down in it, are not only false, but too absurd to have ever entered the head of a crazy politician before. Even Hobbes would blush to own the author for a disciple. He unites the violence and rage of a republican, with all the enthusiasm and folly of a fanatic. If principles of truth and common sense, however, would not serve his scheme, he could not help that by any other method than by inventing such as would; and this he has done.[8]

Inglis, one could argue, was in the intellectual elite on the side of the loyalists (please attempt to counter argue as there is no study to validate the assumption merely judgement on the merits of his work). So, on all sides of the spectrum with respect to the intellectual elite, as will be further explained with Adams's refutation, Paine is *non-influential*. Paine undoubtedly was significant in the mode of thoughts (how the people, in general, thought) of many, but not of the minds that actually contributed to changes in how governance and law was thought about leading to the General Convention of 1787. *If* there was an affect, *then* it was minimal and short lived.[9] Of the two groups, Paine is in the former.[10]

The latter group, while less substantial *quantitatively*, is far more substantial *qualitatively*. In this era the intellectual elites, such as Adams and Jefferson, towered over the quantity of the former group. As Bailyn articulates:

---

[8] Charles Inglis, *The True Interest of America Impartially State, in Certain Strictures on a Pamphlet Intitled Common Sense* (Philadelphia: Humphreys, 1776).

[9] "John Adams autobiography, part 1, 'John Adams,' through 1776 sheet 23 of 53, January-April 1776," http://www.masshist.org/digitaladams/archive/doc?id=A1_23&bc=%2Fdigital-adams%2Farchive%2Fbrowse%2Fautobio1.php. Paine was able to alter the governance structure of, according to Adams's reflections, "Georgia and Vermont as well as Pennsilvania." Shortly after, these three States fell to Anarchy.

[10] This is not, in any way, conceding to a point that the common pamphleteers were *unreasonable*. According to Bailyn, "the American writers were *profoundly reasonable* people. Their pamphlets convey scorn, anger, and indignation; but *rarely blind hate, rarely panic fear*. They [merely] sought to convince opponents" (p. 18). In this, despite deep inclinations, it is affirmed.

But there is more than amateurism behind the relative crudeness of the artistic efforts in the American pamphlets. For if writers like Adams and Jefferson were amateur pamphleteers, their writings in other ways display formidable literary talents. Jefferson had an extraordinary gift for supple and elegant if abstract expression; it was well known and appreciated at the time. And Adams, seemingly so stolid and unimaginative an embodiment of prosaic virtues, had a basically sensuous apprehension of experience which he expressed in brilliantly idiomatic and figurative prose—but in diary notations and letters. Neither, as pamphleteers, sought literary effects: Jefferson's sole effort is a straightforward if gracefully written political policy statement, and Adams's major piece is a treatise on government. [11]

The two literary pieces referred to are Jefferson's *A Summary View on the Rights of British Americans* and Adams's *Thoughts on Government*.[12] Jefferson's *Summary View* "focused on shifting the relationship between metropolis and provinces from one of empire to one of union."[13] In other words, an attempt to mold previous proposals and align colonial legislatures as equal to that of Parliament. This piece, penned in the 1774-1775 era, provided a "less radical, and in some cases, more nuanced...scheme" than many pleas to the Crown that predated the *Summary View*.[14] In respect to the *Thoughts on Government*, Adams first

---

[11] Bailyn, *The Ideological Origins of the American Revolution*, 16.

[12] Thomas Jefferson, *Writings* (New York: The Library of America, 1984), 105-122; "Thoughts on Government," https://www.masshist.org/publications/apde2/view?&id=PJA04dg2; Also see footnote 20 in Bailyn, *The Ideological Origins of the American Revolution*, 16.

[13] Alison LaCroix, *The Ideological Origins of American Federalism* (Cambridge, Massachusetts & London, England: Harvard University Press, 2010), 113.

[14] Ibid, 111. The *Summary View* is contrasted with Cartwright's *American Independence the Interest and Glory of Great Britain* and Galloway's *Plan of a Proposed Union between Great Britain and the Colonies*. For Cartwight the solution to mend the tensions between England and the colonies would be that "Britain would benefit more from a consensual

wrote of the pamphlet to James Warren on April 20 1776,[15] and soon after it gained the widespread recognition of the intellectual elites— the ones that establish government and law.[16]

In lieu of this dichotomy[17], it is imperative to understand that most of the revolutionary moments in the mind of man, with respect to governance and law, that manifested in the Early American Republic came from the latter group: the intellectual elite. Thus, it is justly so that the works of Paine and the other polemicists within this group be negated from further inquiry and analyses with respect to governance and law; and, more materially related, with respect to federalism.

The Data of Literature, Sources, and Modes of Thought: 1760s-1790s
This section will proceed on three different strands: the commons, the philosophy of nature, and governance and law. One may ask, given the substance of the section last, why to include the literature of the commons. The rationale is twofold: the significance of these polemicists ought never be underplayed nor over emphasized. There must be acceptance of the influence of the extravagant works penned on liberty, religion, and the nature of things. Secondly, it also ought to be kept in mind that there is a crucial distinction to

---

league with independent American states." Galloway, on the other hand, it was "formalizing the important legislative role that the colonial assemblies played." Whereas Jefferson, sought to bind the colonies to the Crown as distinct and separate from Parliament. Notwithstanding the call for confederation in all proposals, Jefferson's was viewed as "less radical, and in some cases, more nuanced," and proved a catalyst for reaching the level of Adams within the intellectual elite thusly. Only one caveat, and this is not to concede any points about the *Summary View*, but Jefferson notes that his piece was sent to the Continental Congress and "was read…approved by many, but thought too bold for the present state of things." Notwithstanding, the piece was published and widely distributed in the colonies and England to the point of prominence that it solicited the scrutiny of Edmund Burke: see *Ibid*, 105-120.

[15] "John Adams to James Warren, April 20, 1776," https://www.masshist.org/publications/apde2/view?&id=PJA04d062#ptrPJA04d062n3.

[16] "Thoughts on Government," https://www.masshist.org/publications/apde2/view?&id=PJA04dg2.

[17] This dichotomy, while it began as a discovery, is overshadowed by Elkins and McKitrick as far as they discover a "striking parallel between the Court-Country divisions of Georgian England and those that subsequently appeared in Washington America." Thus, this dichotomy continuously holds constant throughout this vast time period. Elkins and McKitrick, *The Age of Federalism*, 18.

be made on rhetoric of the polemicists and reality of the times that the intellectual elite were operating in and the works they saw as influential. The commons provide insight into the day-to-day passions of the people changing and challenging the wisdom of old. The philosophy of nature shows the paradigm shift within the minds of mankind. It shows a fundamental challenge to the nature of things. The governance and law strand shows a fierce discontent with the status quo around the monarchial world, but also an enlightened and generous challenge to the King-in-Parliament (this was *de facto* parliament but with absolute authority; hence the colloquial term).

To provide brief context, colonial lives—extending to American lives after the Treaty of Paris in 1783—were distant, rural, or concentrated factions within cities, and willingly governed (not controlled) by a ruling class of elites. As the Collier brothers articulate:

> What was life like for Americans in 1787? To begin with, it was mainly rural. Cities were small. Only New York and Philadelphia had populations over 25,000 people. Not more than 10 percent of the population lived in anything that could be called a city or town. By the time of the Convention only 5.4 percent of the population lived in places of 2,500 people or more. Ninety percent of white American men were farmers. Indeed, Jackson Turner Main has calculated that most American men in 1776 owned a farm and those who did not, worked on one. Main's breakdown is this: 40 percent made their livings working on their own farms. Another 30 percent worked as laborers on farms owned by others. Another, smaller, group of men owned large commercial farms or plantations. Finally, the 10 percent or so of American men who were professionals, businessmen, or urban artisans—lawyers, importers, printers—frequently

owned modest farms…in 1787 the typical human
being was a farmer.[18]

Moreover, the predominately rural people stretched across the largest
region of polity in this era and they were "far more rigidly stratified."
Again, the Collier brothers provide context for the workings of the
American life:

> In most communities there existed a small group of
> men who made the basic decisions for the village or
> town, and who were more or less automatically
> elected to legislatures, judgeships, and the like. The
> establishment included large landowners, like Wash-
> ington and Jefferson, wealthy merchants and ship-
> pers, lawyers, and in the North, ministers and
> theologians. There was room for bright young men
> to rise…so that there was always a lowborn in office.[19]

This style in the lives of the Early American Republic was not resented.
In fact, many from the commons ilk felt it just for those learned to
lead, deliberate, and govern the polity. Pragmatically this makes ever
so much sense. As the Collier brothers highlight, "Farmer Jones had
quite enough on his hands with his family, his fields, his woodlots: he
was willing to let the Madisons and Pinckneys worry about running
things—unless the gentlemen went too far and taxed him into poverty,
as they had in Massachusetts."[20] My psychology and philosophy friends
will recognize this as the concept of rational ignorance.

---

[18] Christopher Collier and James Collier, *Decisions in Philadelphia: The Constitutional Convention of 1787* (New York: Ballantine Books, 2007), 22-23.

[19] Collier and Collier, *Decisions in Philadelphia*, 21-22.

[20] *Ibid*, 22. This issue of over taxation and fiscal crisis from centralized governments, wherever they lie, through monetary speculation and lack of hard species to support the speculation, persisted all throughout from the Court-Country divide to the Washington America era. See Elkins and McKitrick, *The Age of Federalism*, 1-131; Jack Rakove, *James Madison and the Creation of the American Republic*, 19-44. For speculation from individuals and those running the Bank of North America prior to the Convention see David Stewart, *The Summer of 1787*, 34.

It is self-evident that the understanding of "the people" was severally fractioned off and the majority classified as commons (this is not an insult but a reality) for rather pragmatic reasons. It is, again, from the totality of the aforementioned, self-evident that there was a dichotomy between the polemicist commons that had the passion of "the people," and the intellectual elite that would *de facto* be the minds behind the design of the Early American Republic's governance system and laws.

The literature of the commons, and proto-elite (akin to Paine),[21] were multifaceted and penned on a multitude of topics. As Bailyn shows, the facades ranged all the way from "Homer, Sophocles, [and] Plato" to "Caeser, the lawyers Ulpain and Gaius, and Justinian, among the Romans."[22] Literature on governance, law, liberty, and the nature of things were so widespread and cherished that the publications found their way into Last Wills to be property transitioned to family. As Josiah Quincy Jr.'s Last Will in 1774 states, "I give to my son when he shall arrive to the age of fifteen years, Algernon Sidney's works,— John Locke's works,—Lord Bacon's works,—Gordon's *Tacitus*,—and *Cato's Letters*. May the spirit of liberty rest upon him!"[23]

Of the aforementioned sources of literature only *Cato's Letters* is really needed to grasp the themes of the collect (disagree if you want, but provide reasoned, cited rebuttals and not just criticism). From the outset, Volume II of *Cato's Letters* authoritatively declares that rampant wickedness, unjust conduct, and mischief has plagued the world (very religiosity modes of reasoning). The first passage is thusly:

> Sir, while I have been reading Hiftory, or cofidering
> the State of humane Affairs, how wofully they are

---

[21] By "proto-elite" I merely mean the medium voices and minds between the commons oscillated by Paine, and the intellectual elite that we view as the framers and founders of our polity. Here I will make a quick transition, since I have provided the distinctions and reality that the intellectual elite (protos will be closely associated though they are not the main source for our inferences to be drawn from) were not endearing to Paine's work, from discussing the commons to the proto-elite and then the intellectual elite.

[22] Bailyn, *The Ideological Origins*, 24. Bailyn quoting Charles Mullett, "Classical Influences on the American Revolution," et al.

[23] Last Will and Testament of Josiah Quincy Jr., 1774. As block quoted in Bailyn, *The Ideological Origins*, 22.

neglected, how foolifhly managed, or how wickedly difconcerted and confounded, in the moft and beft Countries: When I have remembered how large, every where, is the Source of Mifchief, how eafily it is fet a running, and how plentifully it flows; how it is daily breaking into new Channels, and yet none of the old ones are ever fuffered to wax dry; I have been apt to wonder, that the general Condition of Mankind, tho' already vaftly unhappy, is not ftill worfe.[24]

The *Letters* are strongly penned attacks upon the common order. Especially with the English common order. To qualify, the *Letters* went as far as to acknowledge the deceit and tyranny of the Papacy when Rome had consolidated power, but seemingly has, in the context of that time frame, a deeper-seated anger towards the "Root of the Evil [that] still remains" after the Reformation.[25] In volume II of *Letters* alone, one will find 162 references to liberty from tyranny—*of* the mind and *from* the state. Little, if none, can be extrapolated with respect to governance and law.

Within these works, like that of the *Letters*, copious volumes are penned on liberty and the nature of things. Now at this juncture, one will find themselves in bewilderment by now as to what constitutes "the nature of things." With the Enlightenment and the new fascination with deductive logic to find truth (stems from the Great Revolution and era of scientific reasoning seen in Bacon, Newton, etc) there was a fundamental alteration in the substantive conclusions that the masses drew (alter the means; most cases alter the ends). This, as with many things, prompted the challenges of *all* previously held beliefs. Quite literally, this era found widespread fundamental challenges into absolutism type questions. Questions such as, "what is life?" and more material "what is the role of government?" As Alan Kors eloquently

---

[24] [John Trenchard and Thomas Gordon], Cato's Letters, vol. 2 (London: W. Wilkins, T. Woodward, J. Walthoe, and J. Peele, 1723).

[25] *Ibid*, 5.

demonstrates, there was an intellectual innovation (reason and science) and pragmatic devolution (governance became very difficult) into understanding the nature of things. Political and social "revolutions" occur frequently, but a revolution in the mind is transformational and can alter entire governance structures.[26] Thus, proven to revolutionize the ruling ideas of all while at the same time destabilizing the polities.

Ergo, it is understandable to get lost in the rhetoric, logic, and substance of what so many are discussing—what so many are challenging. Very little in this category of the commons and proto-elite can one find serious workings on governance and law. Thus, it is illusory to ascertain that these works can illuminate the wonder of American governance and law of this time. To address, then, Pauline Maier's criticism[27] of Gordon Wood's judgement on the Constitution in his *Creation of the American Republic*, although he may not have articulated this point, it is rather evident that in reality the works of those like Paine and *Cato's Letters*, no matter how much emphasis Bailyn puts upon them,[28] the proposition cannot withstand scrutiny and they had no material effect on the Constitution, governance, or law of the Early American Republic.

The query, then, is advanced to what sources, authors, and works can the scholars of the Early American Republic revert for a proper understand governance and law. "Drawing upon a comprehensive list of political writings by Americans published between 1760 and 1805," Donald Lutz provides, "the study [that] uses a citation count drawn from these 916 items as a surrogate measure of the relative influence of European writers upon American political thought during the era."[29] The data is overwhelmingly in favor of four influential minds

---

[26] The Great Lecture Series, *The mind of the enlightenment*, cassette tapes of lectures by Alan Kors at the University of Pennsylvania, 1991.

[27] See footnote 2 and 7 within this chapter.

[28] See chapters 1 and 2 of Bailyn, *The Ideological Origins of the American Revolution*, 1-54.

[29] Donald Lutz, "The Relative Influence of European Writers on Late Eighteenth-Century American Political Thought," *The American Political Science Review*, Vol. 78, No. 1 (1984): 189-197. I have cataloged, and formulated, his data and will be using it

on the framers and founders of our governance and laws. The four being Montesquieu, Sir William Blackstone, Locke, and Hume, whom all show up indirectly in the *Federalist Papers* and *Anti-Federalist Papers*. In respect to the intellectual elite, this is strikingly coherent in that Jefferson in a letter to Thomas Mann Randolph held:

> The study of the law is useful in a variety of points of view. It qualifies a man to be useful to himself, to his neighbors, and to the public. It is the most certain stepping stone to preferment in the political line. In political oeconomy I think Smith's wealth of nations the best book extant. In the science of government Montesquieu's spirit of laws is generally recommended. It contains indeed a great number of political truths; but almost an equal number of political heresies: so that the reader must be constantly on his guard. There has been lately published a letter of Helvetius who was the intimate friend of Montesquieu and whom he consulted before the publication of his book. Helvetius advised him not to publish it: and in this letter to a friend he gives us a solution for the mixture of truth and error found in this book. He sais Montesquieu was a man of immense reading, that he had commonplaced all his reading, and that his object was to throw the whole contents of his commonplace book into systematical order, and to shew his ingenuity by reconciling the contradictory facts it presented. Locke's little book on government is perfect as far as it goes. *Descending from theory to practice there is no better book than the Federalist.*[30](emphasis added)

---

to show the influence that few had on the intellectual elite. The few that ought to dominate the historical discipline of the Early American Republic.

[30] Letter from Thomas Jefferson to Thomas Mann Randolph, Jr., 30 May 1790: https://founders.archives.gov/documents/Jefferson/01-16-02-0264.

Influence of Most Cited Thinkers

- Montesquieu
- Blackstone
- Locke
- Hume
- Plutarch
- Beccaria
- Trenchard & Gordon
- Delolme
- Pufendorf
- Coke
- Cicero
- Hobbes
- Robertson
- Grotius
- Rousseau
- Bolingbroke
- Bacon
- Price
- Shakespeare
- Livy
- Pope
- Milton
- Tacitus
- Coxe
- Plato
- Abbe Raynal
- Mably
- Machiavelli

Figure 1. Influence of Most Cited Thinkers: Total numbers of citations is 3,154; Total number of thinkers is 76.

Thus, when Elkins and McKitrick in *The Age of Federalism* hold that the works of *The Independent Whig*, *The Craftsman*, and *Cato's Letters* made "so profound an impression in America,"[31] and Maier's criticism of Wood negating the influence of Paine on the Constitution; it is a notion that is not applicable to the framers and founders of the Constitution, governance systems, and laws of the Early American Republic; those that qualitatively matter.

The Consequences of Literature, Sources, and Modes of Thought in the Early American Republic
In the Early American Republic there are, at least, three broad areas of revolutionary alterations in the mind of mankind. The first is in respect to representation and consent of the governed. Secondly, within the framework of "the nature of things," there was fundamental shifts in constitutional thought and rights. Lastly, and the most contentious of the colonials throughout the Stamp Act Crisis and extending into the

---

[31] Elkins and McKitrick, *The Age of Federalism*, 6.

late era of the Early American Republic, came the element "that the Revolution was fought" over: Sovereignty.[32] Thus, of these three the greatest is sovereignty; and the last two are the material elements for understanding divided authority federalism.[33]

Colonial understanding of the unwritten English constitution changed in the 1760s. James Otis may be credited with commencing this paradigm shift.[34] Notwithstanding, the real changes did not ferment until the 1770s in colonial America. John Adams was the first distinguished colonial who viewed the unwritten English constitution as "a frame, a scheme, a system, a combination of powers."[35] Sometime after this point is when the paradigm shift occurred throughout the colonies and England. By the mid-1770s, Inglis echoes Adams's perspective on the constitution:

> What is the constitution that word so often used— so little understood—so much perverted? It is, as I conceive—*that assemblage of laws, customs, and institutions which from the general system according to which the several powers of the state are distributed and their respective rights are secured* to the different members of the community.[36] (emphasis added)

---

[32] Bailyn, *The Ideological Origins of the American Revolution*, 198.

[33] The first transformational is not necessarily material for the purposes of understanding federalism with respect to governance structure and law. It is also, as Bailyn highlights, a rather complex element to the equation. Further research and a separate thesis will be needed to analyze this element in grave detail. For contemporary federalism scholars this portion would fit into the "Principle-Agent" inquiry.

[34] See in general *Ibid*, 175-198.

[35] Bailyn quoting John Adams in *Ibid*, 175.

[36] Inglis, *The True Interest of America Impartially Stated, in Certain Strictures on a Pamphlet Intitled Common Sense*, as quoted in Bailyn, *The Ideological Origins of the American Revolution*, 175. Hon. Ted Cruz (R-TX), on many things am I inclined to agree with you, but with respect to institutional rights for institutional powers conferred by the people over an extended republic, I cannot. The Hon. Cruz articulated in his Princeton University undergrad thesis, *Clipping the Wings of Angels: The History and Theory Behind the Ninth and Tenth Amendments to the United States Constitution*, that "the Ninth Amendment addresses 'rights,' and the Tenth, the distribution of 'powers.' Yet, repeatedly, politicians, scholars, judges, even Framers confuse the two." Whereas I am in agreement that each concept is distinct, I cannot share the false assertion that "it is

After this, it became the dominant understanding, along with the loose framework of the powers and structures, there was a desire for a written constitution. The intrinsic notions of a constitution changed, thusly. It was no longer conceived as an unwritten document premised on traditions and open to alterations—as whomever in power saw fit. Instead, there was a desire for codified principles to be instantiated and only through a super-majority undone.

Finally, the greatest of the three was over sovereignty, dominion, the authority conferred. The first two were "basic problems, considerations of which led to shifts in thought," but the "intellectual problems the colonists faced" of critical importance dealt with "the idea of sovereignty."[37] As will be discussed in far more detail throughout this book, sovereignty shifted from sovereignty in a "body absolute and arbitrary," to the "*whole* body of people," and finally to divided sovereignties within certain spheres of conferred and delegated powers.[38]

---

meaningless for a government to have rights over people, for a government right is simply a legitimate power." Why? Simply stated, it is just as possible for "individuals" to galvanize through a traveling faction, much like Carrie Nation in the progressive era, to circumvent the structure, rights, and powers that are imbedded in our Constitution and history thereof. Could a faction like that seen in the 18th amendments' progressive era roots take away the bulwarks of a stable democratic-republic? No.

[37] *Ibid*, 198.

[38] For "body absolute and arbitrary": Thomas Hobbes, *Leviathan* (London: Penguin Books, 1985), 228-239. Also see, Sir William Blackstone, *Commentaries on the laws of England*, (Chicago: Forgotten Books, 2012), 39. For "whole body of people": James Otis, *Rights of the British Colonies* (JHL 7). Also see, Bailyn, *The Ideological Origins of the American Revolution*, 205. For "divided sovereignties": LaCroix, *The Ideological Origins of American Federalism*, in general; Berger, *Federalism: The Founder's Design*, in general.

CHAPTER II

Brief History of the Antecedents of Federalism

A Series of occurrences, many recent events…afford great reason to believe that a deep-laid and desperate plan of imperial despotism has been laid, and partly executed, for the extinction of all civil liberty…The august and once revered fortress of English freedom—the admirable work of ages—the BRITISH CONSTITU-TION seems fast tottering into fatal and inevitable ruin. The dreadful catastrophe threatens universal havoc, and presents an awful warning to hazard all if, peradventure, we in these distant confines of the *earth may prevent being totally overwhelmed and buried* under the ruins of our most established rights.

—Boston Town Meeting
to its Assembly Representatives, 1770

Defining Federalism

For clarity, the working definition of federalism will be explained throughout this section, and then conclude with the accepted and proper definition. To be clear, the epicenter of federalism is division. Interdisciplinary scholars of federalism, though few—from non-legal historians, to political scientists, to legal historians—are all ascertaining the same principled concept. Federalism is divided authority.

The Collier brothers, non-legal historians, skirt around federalism, but if one looks to their work, *Decisions in Philadelphia*, it is evident they provide their idea of the concept.[39] Their understanding is political divisions. Elkins and McKitrick, prominent non-legal historians,

---

[39] Collier, *Decision in Philadelphia: The Constitutional Convention of 1787*, index 425 and 121-127.

seemingly view federalism as more of a social *and* political construct. Although, towards the end of their book, they seem to associate federalism exclusively with the Federalist Party; which would manifest under Hamiltonians, to offset the Jeffersonians.

Thus, there was more social association under the guise of political scheming. To political scientist and democratic theorist, Robert Dahl, federalism is "states, provinces, or cantons...[that] are not simply legal creatures of the central government with boundaries and powers that the central government could, in principle, modify as it chooses. They are basic elements in the constitutional design and in the political life of the country."[40] Thus, Dahl conceptualizes institutional structure and a political structure for federalism—he does not go beyond this and erroneously assumes states are subservient.[41] In other words, Dahl understands the necessity for multiplicity but sees the need as a consequence of the nature of politics: factions predating on others for power. But erroneously asserts that there is no divided authority vertically (between the States and the federal head).

Legal historians along with the non-legal historian Garry Wills, if pressed, would derive the conclusion that federalism has a natural formulation that encompasses all of the aforementioned concepts. A consequence of which is an institutional structure to prevent what necessitated its formulation, or to maintain what was needed. This natural formulation is not a normative affirmation that federalism should be moldable, or living, it is a testament to the raw power and respect federalism commands. Federalism either begins or ends with institutional divisions of authority. If it begins with institutional divisions, then when those divisions decay social revolts culminate. If it ends with institutional divisions, then social revolts are the direct causation of federalism manifesting. It would either be the decay of federalism—

---

[40] Robert Dahl, *How Democratic is the American Constitution?*, 44-45. Dahl highlights the limitations of the federal government and necessity of the States. Some may conceptualize this relation (federal and State) as vertical federalism. Dahl views this as the Constitution's "admirable brevity" premised on "structures, powers, and rights."

[41] For a broad understanding of how the political science discipline views federalism see Angerholzer III, et al., *Triumphs and Tragedies of the Modern Presidency: Case Studies in Presidential Leadership* (California and Colorado: Praeger, 2016), 192. "The political relationship between national government and the states...known as federalism."

and the rule of law—that would cause despotism and social tumult, as in the cases of Colonial America and Nazi Germany.[42] Or, the result of social revolt is federalism; which was the case for Latin colonies settled by Britain, after becoming a global power in 1815.[43] Somewhere in between the former and latter is the true loci of federalism. Thus, no matter which lens attached, time or place, to those that study federalism, the epicenter is always dividing authority.

If it be correct that the epicenter of federalism is division, then it must follow that division is the crux of the concept. Federalism, then, has a "core idea of divided governmental authority."[44] It must be, in some form, the "distribution of powers between the federal government and the States."[45] Garry Wills shows an intellectual understanding on par with LaCroix. Wills demonstrates the multiplicity of federalism, not only with the institutional system the framers created, but of the natural formulation of the concept. Notwithstanding, Wills does not explicitly articulate this understanding. Instead he breaks down the different understandings of the same concept. To Wills, mixed government means "divisions of forces in terms of *interests*," and separation of powers means "division of forces in terms of *function*."[46] The concept of mixed government and separation of powers can be found in the structure of Congress. The lower chamber represents the vast *interests*: the people's chamber. The upper chamber represents the *functions*: check on federal government by the States and check on each branch in the bicameral system. The concept of separation of powers can be seen in that the lower house has the sole right of originating appropriation bills while the upper cannot usurp this right.[47] Are not all substantive examples of

---

[42] See in general Elkins and McKitrick, *The Age of Federalism*, 17-18. "The sacred balance of the Constitution, the venerable equilibrium of king, lords, and commons, was teetering over an abyss of corruption"; Michael Stolleis, *The Law Under the Swastika* (Chicago and London: The University of Chicago Press, 1998), 1-40, 48-102.

[43] Benton and Ford, *Rage for Order* (Cambridge and London: Harvard University Press, 2016), 1-18, 28-55, and 164-169. Many Latin colonies confederalized into "firm leagues of friendship."

[44] LaCroix, *The Ideological Origins of American Federalism*, 11.

[45] Raoul Berger, *Federalism: The Founder's Design* (Norman and London: University of Oklahoma Press, 1987), 3.

[46] Garry Wills, *The Federalist Papers* (New York: Bantam Book, 1982), introduction.

these concepts divided authority?

Is federalism social, political, or institutional making it legal principles thusly? Federalism, to be sure, is not some "transcendent notion that was always available to canny national builders."[48] In respect for this book's purpose, LaCroix's understanding that federalism is an "artifact of intellectual endeavor at a particular historical moment" is accepted.[49] If this be so, then the history of federalism furnishes the definition. As the brief literature review from above, across disciplines, shows; federalism at its core is divided authority. This is the understanding in its most reduced form. In the most comprehensive and accurate form federalism is: multiplicity of polities with different interests, collected under one compact, over an extended republic, with institutional divisions within respected spheres of sovereignty that cannot be usurped, commandeered, or abrogated by the conflicting sovereign; all in which have vertical and horizontal checks on usurpation.

A Summary of the Historical Antecedents of Federalism: Non-Colonial Perspective

Federalism, as exhaustively defined, seemingly makes its first institutional formulation of note in the Union of Crowns. The Union of Crowns not only shows the first *institutional* formulation, but shows the necessity of divided authority on *interests* principles as evident of the Union's fall. LaCroix is correct to commence her analysis of federalism with the Union of Crowns.[50] The charge of Gordon Wood that LaCroix's *The Ideological Origins of American Federalism* is "based on often *odd readings* of an extensive body of primary and secondary sources"[51] is one that, at least with respect to the Union of Crowns, is not sustainable.

[47] Art. I §1-2, *United States Constitution*, http://avalon.law.yale.edu/18th_century/art1.asp.

[48] LaCroix, *The Ideological Origins of American Federalism*, 6.

[49] *Ibid*

[50] The careful reader will say she did not commence her analysis here, but a careful reader will counter that the first two sections in her The Federal Idea chapter are of theory. In respect to practice, she correctly commences with the Union of Crowns—the most substantive example.

[51] Gordon Wood, "Federalism from the Bottom Up," *The University of Chicago Law Review* 78 (2011): 706.

The Union of Crowns was the accumulation of the England empire and of Scotland in 1603. King James the VI of Scots and eventually the I of England did not think like the normal kingships of his time. At a young age King James the VI and I's tutor was the "classical Scholar and reformer George Buchanan."[52] A young King James the VI and I had the typical schooling of any noble of the era. But he had an atypical understanding of the history of "political theories on kingship."[53] For King James VI and I it was evident that "since time immemorial, kingship had depended on a contract between king and people: the people, who appointed one of their number as their ruler, retained their inalienable rights to life, liberty[,] and property."[54] This posed a strict contradiction to contemporary wisdom, especially the traditional wisdom in Britain of a divine unitary sovereignty. Additionally, this shows an *interests* principle understanding of federalism: checks on the Crown by the people. Though it would not ferment in the Union of Crowns.

As Magnus Magnusson highlights, "the accession of James VI of Scotland and James I of England had created the Union of the Crowns in 1603."[55] On March 24, 1603, Queen Elizabeth of England died without naming a successor to the throne of England. With Sir Robert Cecil "in secret correspondence with King James VI" for ascendency to the throne, letter quickly reached him in Scotland of Elizabeth's death. As noted in the *Tales of a Grandfather*:

> The breath had no sooner left Elizabeth's body, than the near relation and godson of the late Queen, Sir Robert Carey, got on horseback, and, travelling with a rapidity which almost equaled that of the modern mail-coach, carried to the Palace of Holyrood the news that James was King

---

[52] Magnus Magnusson, *Scotland: The Story of a Nation* (New York: Grove Press, 2000), 383.

[53] *Ibid*, 384.

[54] *Ibid*.

[55] *Ibid*, 537.

of England, France and Ireland, as well as of his native dominions of Scotland.[56]

Notwithstanding the ascendency of King James the VI and I, the Union of Crowns "united the kingdoms only to the extent that it gave them 'one Head or Sovereign'; it did not unite them in one body politic."[57] Thus, there was an *institutional* principle of federalism with two legislative bodies under one head.

The Union of Crowns, however, could not last. The culture differences proved too vast and there was little care to govern the separate *interests* of the Court and the Gaelic country accordingly.[58] By 1609 policies were enacted to curtail the social revolts. Or really, they were to "bring the Highlands and Islands to civility."[59] Notwithstanding the attempt for union, the idea was inevitable to fail without a system to govern the separate interests. The Glorious Revolution of 1689 was the fall of the union. In England it was viewed as glorious because the union dissolved without bloodshed, but in Scotland it flowed from the Highlands. As Magnusson highlights:

> Since the Union of the Crowns in 1603, the Scots had been under kings who had forced on them a choice they did not want—between their religious allegiance to Presbyterianism and their political allegiance to the Stewart dynasty. This had led to a century of struggle and conflict.[60]

---

[56] Sir Walter Bart, *Tales of a Grandfather* (Edinburgh: Constable Printer to Her Majesty), chapter XXXIII.

[57] Brian Levack, *The Formation of the British State: England, Scotland, and the Union, 1603-1707* (Oxford: Clarendon Press, 1987), 1. Also quoted in LaCroix, *The Ideological Origins of American Federalism*, 25.

[58] Magnusson, *Scotland: The Story of a Nation*, 404-417. This chapter also notes how far more legitimate the union was perceived from the vantage of England.

[59] *Ibid*, 407. Magnusson quoting Michael Lynch.

[60] *Ibid*, 511.

Thus, after a rocky duration of meddling with the concept we now call federalism the Union fell because of an inability to permit divided governmental *institutional* authority over an extended union with respect to negation of *interests* principles.

The history of federalism, though, has a more substantial theoretical backdrop.[61] One that can be found in piecemeal collections of the most circulated and studied philosophes and legal theorists of the seventeenth and eighteenth centuries. LaCroix is correct in stating:

> Beginning with the work of Hugo Grotius in the early seventeenth century and continuing with the writing of Samuel Von Pufendrof in the later seventeenth century and Emmerich de Vattel in the mideighteenth century, a long line of European thinkers had offered an alternative to the English (later, British) all-or-nothing, unitary vision of sovereignty and the belief that multiple sovereignties necessarily spelled solecism and disaster.[62]

The very idea of divided authority federalism was repugnant to the English common law. The leading authority Blackstone declared:

> The power and jurisdiction of parliament…is so transcendent and absolute that it cannot be confined either for causes or persons, within any bounds. It hath sovereignty and uncontrollable authority in the making, confirming, enlarging, restraining, abrogating,

---

[61] A point should be made to not, as LaCroix and Wood discuss, graft these ideas into the historiographical understanding of the Union of Crowns or in the proceedings before the General Convention and the ratification debates. John Adams and some of the earliest founders used the Union as precedent, but one cannot find any call of federalism within the historiography of the Union. The evidence, however, and mode of thought found in the big data analytics (revert to the graphs throughout this thesis) should grant significant weight to the correlations between the Union, the Early American Republic, and federalism. In statistical terminology, perhaps moving to a 90th percentile probability rate, although this would be impossible to quantitatively measure. The relation is almost intuitive.

[62] LaCroix, *The Ideological Origins of American Federalism*, 18.

> repealing, reviving, and expounding of laws...this
> being the place where that absolute despotic power,
> which must in all governments reside somewhere,
> is intrusted by the constitution of these kingdoms.[63]

What is absolutely striking is that this was not Blackstone's only mention of sovereignty. It would also happen to be that Jefferson, and the other colonials, in his *Summary View* exploited this second mentioning of sovereignty to strengthen their arguments for divided authority federalism. The leading authority Blackstone also declared:

> And, first, the law ascribes to the king the attribute
> of sovereignty or pre-eminence. Hence it is, that no
> suit or action can be brought against the king, even
> in civil matters, because no court can have jurisdic-
> tion over him. For all jurisdiction implies superiority
> of power.[64]

Notwithstanding, the English and loyalists held on to the notion that Parliament is the sovereign and to hold otherwise would be illogical; it would be a solecism. By solecism was also referred to as *Imperium in Imperio*, or sovereign within a sovereign, and this was against the consensus thought. The unstudied and odd contradiction here is the leading authority, Blackstone. While belittling divided authority federalism as a solecism, he found one unwittingly within the English system. Few philosophes and legal theorists through their "intellectual endeavor" ended up paving the road for the framers of the United States Constitution to create federalism and negate the solecism that seemingly was always there.

Predating the Early American Republic the few philosophes and legal theorists provided the cornerstones for what we now know as federalism to manifest. There were three, at least, minds

---

[63] Blackstone, *Commentaries on the laws of England*, 39.

[64] *Ibid*, 49.

that are directly related to the apriori formulation of federalism.[65] The three minds are Hugo Grotius, Samuel von Pufendorf, and James Hodges. For a brief time frame for this portion of the analysis; the scene for these three are in the mid to late seventeenth century with Hodges's theory being accepted in the Act of Union of 1707: another precedent. LaCroix succinctly articulates Grotius and Pufendorf's theories:

> The Grotian view of the law of nations emphasized what Edward Keene terms an "extra-European order" of colonial and imperial systems based on "the principle that sovereignty should be divided across national and territorial boundaries." Pufendorf's *Law of Nature and Nations* (1672) offered a similar vision of nonunitary authority based on his study of the German Empire. By the mid-seventeenth century, that empire had been reduced essentially to an elective monarchy. Centralized sovereignty, if it had ever existed, had been replaced by satellite princes, each husbanding his own store of authority over his own territory.[66]

It is self-evident that these two theories divided the polities authorities; the polities sovereignty. This can either be conceptualized as "top down" federalism. Or, one can conceptualize this as manifesting in some "natural formulation"[67] from the middle, branching outward. Notwithstanding, the Act of Union of 1707 emulates James Hodges understanding of an "incorporating union." This form of union is seen more closely in the Union of Crowns: two distinct sovereigns incorporating under one.

---

[65] Apriori in the sense that Grotius, Pufendorf, and Hodges seemingly only had observations from their studies and deductively reasoned their way to federalism. This also follows from what we now know from the mode of thought as seen in chapter one.

[66] LaCroix, *The Ideological Origins of American Federalism*, 19.

[67] Revert to the section "Defining Federalism" in Part two.

A Summary of the Historical Antecedents of Federalism: Colonial Perspective
Federalism at its core is divided authority. If this is understood and
the totality of the aforementioned strengthens this notion, then there
is some natural formulation behind federalism. It is one that was discovered and driven by ideas and experiences stretched over time. If
federalism is not exclusively seen, though brought to its best form, in
the Early American Republic, then it cannot follow, as Gordon Wood
contends, that the colonists "learned [from] the beginning that political authority was divisible and created from the bottom up."[68] If that
proposition be true, then would scholars not be in effect erasing the
lines of the very first charters? The Charter of the Massachusetts Bay
Colony (1629) states:

> CHARLES, BY THE GRACE OF GOD, Kinge of
> England,...&c, TO ALL to whome theis Presents
> shall come Greeting...knowe yee...Wee...give and
> graunte unto...Sir Henry Rosewell, Sir John
> Younge, Sir Richard Saltonstall...all that Parte of
> Newe England in America, which lyes...between a
> great River there, comonlie called Monomack River,
> alias Merrimack Rivier, and certen other River
> there, called Charles River, being in the Bottom of
> a certain Bay there, comonlie called Massachu-
> setts...*there shalbe one Governor, one Deputy Governor,*
> *and eighteene Assistants of the same Company, to be from*
> *tyme to tyme constituted, elected and chosen out of*
> *Freemen of the saide Company...one great generall and*
> *solempe assemblie, which foure generall assemblies shalbe*
> *stiled and called the foure greate and general courts...*
> *WEE DOE...graaunte to the said Governor and Com-*
> *pany...full power and authorite to choose...And to make*
> *Lawes and Ordinaces for the Good and Welfare...soe as*
> *such Lawes and ordinaces be contrarie or repugnant to*

---

[68] Wood, "Federalism from the Bottom Up," 711.

the Lawes and Statuts of this our Realme of England.[69]
(emphasis added)

Notwithstanding the vast experiences the colonies had with what would be seen in contemporary times as local government,[70] there was always a centralized government housed in the separate and independent States under the sovereign of the Crown. Thus, it cannot be accepted that federalism permeated from the people in a bottom-up manner and was known and established from the beginning. LaCroix summarizes the true antecedents of federalism, from the colonial perspective, as properly defined:

> The [Stamp Act] Debates of the 1760s through the 1780s culminated in a new constitutionalization of federalism, a process that continued into the 1800s. From a disconnected and sometimes ambiguous set of arguments about divided sovereignty in politics, American colonists and early republicans fashioned a new architecture of legal and constitutional authority built on a subject matter division of governmental power. In contrast to earlier systems— whether formal or informal—of polycentric government, the federalism of the late eighteenth- and

---

[69] Michael Benedict, *Sources in American Constitutional History* (New York and London: Rowman and Littlefield, 2016), 8-9.

[70] See in general *Ibid*. Wood provides examples of local polity organization from Jamestown and the Chesapeake to the New England Confederation of 1643. Moreover, Wood holds that under his understanding representation was the controlling issue. If this is so, then how does Wood account for Bailyn's statement on sovereignty shown in Part one? To the author's knowledge he has not. Wood also goes as far as to suggest that X (the totality of LaCroix's evidence) could not be because of Y (the totality of Wood's evidence). As if, somehow, there cannot be multiple pieces to one puzzle. This is untenable with the principles of logic. Since LaCroix addresses Wood point for point, then her position is accepted because it moves to understanding the true concept of federalism, and not some ad hoc examples that does not harm the proposition and in some cases strengthens it (this makes sense to me but probably not to others...we may need to work out the syntax structure). Analyze in conjunction, Wood's "Federalism from the Bottom Up" and LaCroix's "Rhetoric and Reality in Early American Legal History: A Reply to Gordon Wood."

early nineteenth-century United States was specifically designed to avoid the ancient problem of imperium in imperio, or dominion within a dominion,
that had so troubled the British Atlantic political
world for decades. The significant innovation of the
American federal idea was to authorize the division
of sovereignty and to create viable legal categories
that could contain multiple sources of governmental
power within one an overarching system.[71]

The point of inductive inquiry commences with the Stamp Act Debates with the backdrop of the evidence in the non-colonial perspective antecedent history of federalism.[72]

To provide brief context for the contentions manifest in the
Stamp Act Debates: There is a general consensus that colonial America was in a period of salutary neglect from the Mayflower Compact's
body politic in 1620 until the aftermath of the seven years war. It
would be difficult and inaccurate to argue to the contrary, because in
practice they were but it was *artificial* from England's perspective. The
colonial charters, comparatively to the rest of the empire's charters,
were economic liberty grants to settle and foster economic prosperity
in the name of the Crown. Important for federalism, however, is the
institutional legality of the colonies: who held sovereignty. The
Mayflower Compact reads:

> IN THE NAME OF GOD, AMEN. We, whose
> names are underwritten, *the Loyal Subjects of our dread*
> *Sovereign Lord King James*, by the Grace of God, of
> Great Britian...Having undertaken for the Glory of
> God, and Advancement of Christian Faith, and the
> Honour of our King and Country, a Voyage to plant

---

[71] Alison LaCroix, "Rhetoric and Reality in Early American Legal History: A Response
to Gordon Wood," 78 University of Chicago Law Review 733 (2011).

[72] See previous section entitled *A Summary of Historical Antecedents of Federalism: Non-
Colonial Perspective.*

the first Colony in the northern Parts of Virginia; Do by these Presents, solemnly and mutually, in the Presence of God and one another, covenant and combine ourselves together into a civil Body Politick, for our better Ordering and Preservation, and Furtherance of the Ends aforesaid: *And by Virtue hereof do enact, constitute, and frame, such just and equal Laws, Ordinances, Acts, Constitutions, and Officers, from time to time, as shall be thought must meet and convenient for the general Good of the Colony; unto which we promise all due Submission and Obedience.*[73] (emphasis added)

Explicitly within this charter one will see that for pragmatic reasons the colonies established their own laws, but it is also explicit that the Crown retains sole sovereignty. As Blackstone describes, however, Parliament also houses sovereignty with the Crown.

In England, a generation later, it was perceived that the colonists were the cause of the seven years war (whether it is true or not is irrelevant for this purpose). The consequence of such was an attempt to reign in the burdensome colonies.[74] In 1765 Parliament passed the

---

[73] Benedict, *Sources in American Constitutional History*, 11. This should not be construed in such a manner that one believes the almighty force of the Crown colonized the Americas. In fact, the contrary of this is true. In 1607 Royal Governor John Smith colonized Jamestown. Upon landing "twenty or thirty [of his men] went ashore with the captain, and in coming aboard, they were assaulted with certain Indians, which charged them within pistol shot, in which conflict Capt. Archer and Morton were shot, whereupon Cpt Newport seconding them, made a shot at them." A month later Governor Smith's colony was assaulted again by "400 Indians." Governor Smith basically was the king and life force of this very small expeditionary colony. See: John Smith, *A True Relation of Virginia*, 1608. The point to draw is that when governance started to become formalized it is clear that the colonies could intra-legislate—with the contradiction that would soon culminate in the Stamp Act Debates on legislative jurisdiction—but that the Crown and Parliament held dominion. Wood would contend that this localism throughout colonial history is the "experiences" the colonials and then the framers would say drove their mode of thought. One could get lost in events and evidence of this intense local, self-government. Whereas it most certainly had an effect, these were not the only "experiences" they relied on. For clarity on this point revert to Chapter one.

[74] Truth be told, from 1714 to 1739 Parliament promulgated 29 different laws on colonial trade. This was unprecedented and is where the culminating resentment of the intellectual elites for Parliament probably came from—incremental intrusion. From the colonial perspective, the Stamp Act of 1765 and the Coercive and Intolerable Acts of

Stamp Act. The preamble reads:

> An act for granting and applying certain stamp du-
> ties, and other duties, in the British colonies and
> plantations in America, towards further defraying
> the expences of defending, protecting, and securing
> the same; and for amending such parts of the several
> acts of parliament relating to the trade and revenues
> of the said colonies and plantations, as direct the
> manner of determining and recovering the penalties
> and forfeitures therein mentioned.[75]

From the colonial perspective, this attempt was a usurpation on "all the Rights and Liberties of America." The Stamp Act levied a penalty in the form of taxation "for every skin or piece of vellum or parchment, or sheet or piece of paper, on which shall be ingrossed, written or printed, any declaration, plea, replication, rejoinder, demurrer, or other pleading…a stamp duty of three pence." The provisions of the Stamp Act were exhaustive and went as far as to levy four pounds for every piece of parchment used in any licensing transaction with respect to "spirituous liquors" sales.[76]

The colonial resentment to this legislation prompted intense debates into the nature of Parliament's authority now denoted as The Stamp Act Crisis. The diary of John Adams articulates the colonial perspective well:

> In the Course of my Business, as a Surveyor of
> High-Ways, as one of the Committee, for dividing,
> planning, and selling the North-Commons, in the

1774 was the final points of usurpation. It must be noted that the older generation by the time of Coercive and Intolerable Acts would have had the experiences of the 1714-1739 levies. So, this is not a stretch of imagination to ascertain the aforementioned point.

[75] The Stamp Act, March 22, 1765:
http://avalon.law.yale.edu/18th_century/stamp_act_1765.asp.

[76] *Ibid.*

Course of my two great journeys to Pounalborough and Marthas Vineyard, and in several smaller journeys to Plymouth, Taunton and Boston, I had many fine Opportunities and Materials for Speculation.— The Year 1765 has been the most remarkable Year of my Life. That enormous Engine, fabricated by the british Parliament, for battering down all the Rights and Liberties of America, I mean the Stamp Act, has raised and spread, thro the whole Continent, a Spirit that will be recorded to our Honours, with all future Generations. In every Colony, from Georgia to New Hampshire inclusively, the Stamp Distributors and Inspectors have been compelled, by the unconquerable Rage of the People, to renounce their offices. Such and so universal has been the Resentment of the People, that every Man who has dared to speak in favour of the Stamps, or to soften the detestation in which they are held...Connections and Influence had been, has been seen to sink into universal Contempt and Ignominy.[77]

As shown, the Stamp Act manifested a deep and intrinsic resentment to Parliament throughout the colonies amongst all statuses. One that would maintain throughout even after its repeal.

In January 1766, there was a paradigm shift in Parliament to repeal the Stamp Act. Parliament member William Pitt voiced that it was his opinion "that the Stamp Act be repealed absolutely, totally, and immediately...At the same time, let the sovereign authority of this country over the colonies, be asserted in as strong terms as can be devised, and be made to extend to every point of legislation whatsoever."[78] Pitt would go on to make a distinction between "external

---

[77] "John Adams diary 11, 18-29 December 1765": http://www.masshist.org/digital-adams/archive/doc?id=D11&numrecs=2&archive=all&hi=on&mode=&query=1765%2520WEDNESDAY&queryid=&rec=1&start=1&tag=text.

[78] LaCroix, *The Ideological Origins of American Federalism*, 41. Quoting Parliament member William Pitt.

and internal taxes...between taxes levied...and duties imposed."[79] Many historians have been debating many different fine points with respect to the Stamp Act, the debates, and colonial intent on using Pitt's statements to argue for subject matter division of authority to legislate.[80] Notwithstanding the nuances, dividing authority shifts from merely philosophes and legal theorists speculating to becoming entrenched in the vernacular of the colonials and Parliament.

Shortly following the Stamp Act crisis and upheaval in the colonies, which uprooted many Royal officials making governance in the colonies all the worse for the King-in-Parliament[81], the Declaratory Act was passed and addressed the distress of the colonials by repealing the Stamp Act. The Declaratory Act, however, went further and more or less gave incredible soundness to the arguments and fears of the colonists. The Declaratory Act stated:

> Whereas several of the houses of representatives in his Majesty's colonies and plantations in *America*, have of late, *against law, claimed to themselves...the sole and exclusive right of imposing duties and taxes upon his Majesty's subjects in the sad colonies and plantations; and have, in pursuance of such claim, passed certain votes, resolutions, and orders, derogatory to the legislative authority of parliament, and inconsistent with the dependency of the said colonies and plantations upon the crown...the said colonies and plantations in America have been, are, and of right ought to be, subordinate* unto, and <u>*depenmindent*</u> *upon the imperial crown and parliament...* the temporal, and commons...in *parliament assembled, had, hath, and of right ought to have full power and*

---

[79] *Ibid*, 42.

[80] *Ibid*, 42-44.

[81] The reader will notice a language shift here from "Parliament" to the "King-in-Parliament." Throughout the 1760s and 1770s there was an assimilation of powers into one body—the King-in-Parliament. As LaCroix highlights, it was "the corporate legislative entity constituted by the combined authority of the Crown and Parliament" (p. 32).

authority to make laws…in all cases whatsoever…all res-olutions, votes, orders, and proceedings, in any of the said colonies…to make laws…are hereby declared to be, utterly null and void to all intents and purposes whatsoever.[82]
(emphasis added)

This repeal law promulgated what William Pitt opined in that the "sovereign authority" declared the rights to legislate the colonies "in all cases whatsoever."[83] Psychologists will recognize this as the All-or-Nothing paradox. With these Acts and the new concept of the King-in-Parliament the *institutional divisions* dissolved and fostered more tumult among both the colonials and the Brits.

As tensions, debates, and riots exponentially grew; the disdain for the King-in-Parliament grew commensurate (does this remind any-one of any other point of political history?). The consequences of which culminated in 1774 with the debate on federalism shifting from subject matter divisions to the colonial general assembly retaining the same status as the King-in-Parliament with the only sovereign being the Crown. For brief context, this was perceived by the British and loyalists as radical and untenable. It was, therefore, to the British and loyalists, a solecism—as previously defined. It was revolutionary to ascertain that the colonial general assembly could be on par with the King-in-Parliament since sovereignty resided with them. These are the experiences of the colonials that led to independence, the Articles of Confederation, and in part the General Convention. Permit the inquiry and self-reflect: if the vast time frame can render so many changes, paradigm shifts, new generations and biases, then how pow-erful are the elements that remain relatively constant with principles built upon said elements? It must be of substantial historical and in-tellectual significance.

---

[82] Benedict, *Sources in American Constitutional History*, 14.

[83] LaCroix, *The Ideological Origins of American Federalism*, 59.

CHAPTER III —

Divided Authority Federalism Manifests

The State governments possess inherent advantages, which will ever give them an influence and ascendency over the National Government, and will for ever preclude the possibility of federal encroachments. *That their liberties, indeed, can be subverted by the federal head, is repugnant to every rule of political calculation.*

—Alexander Hamilton,
New York Ratification Convention, June 17, 1788

The several states composing the United States of America are *not united on the principle of unlimited submission to their general government; but by a compact under the style and title of a Constitution for the United States, and of amendments thereto, they constituted a general government for special purposes delegated to that government certain definite powers and whensoever the general government assumes undelegated powers, its acts are unauthoritative, void, and of no force.* To this compact each state acceded as a state, and is integral party, its co-states forming, as to itself, the other party. The government created by this compact was not made the exclusive or final judge of the extent of the powers delegated to itself, since that would have made its discretion, and not the Constitution the measure of its powers.

—Thomas Jefferson,
Original Draft of the Kentucky Resolutions, 1798

The Declaration of Independence and the Articles of Confederation
The concluding section in Chapter two discussed in length "the consequences which culminated" and prompted colonial independence in 1774-76. Most tend to stay close to the common phrase in the Declaration of Independence that "we hold these truths to be self-evident: That all men are created equal; that they are endowed by their Creator with certain unalienable rights…to life, liberty, and the pursuit of happiness."[84] It is much like the fascination with the Constitution to only care about "We the People" in the preamble. If only these few words told the whole story then simplicity would actually make sense. The governing principle issue was sovereignty, legislative authority, and by association federalism.[85]

Other than the common phrase of the Declaration of Independence the document also declared:

> Prudence, indeed, will dictate that governments long established should not be changed for light and transient causes; and accordingly *all experience hath shown* that mankind are more disposed to suffer, while evils are sufferable than to right themselves by abolishing the forms to which they are accustomed. *But when a long train of abuses and usurpations,* pursuing invariably the same object, envinces a *design too reduce them under absolute despotism,* it is their right, it is their duty, to *throw off such government, and to provide necessity which constrains them to alter their former systems of government.* The history of the present King of Great Britain is a history of repeated injuries and usurpations, all having in direct object the establishment

---

[84] Declaration of Independence, July 4, 1776: http://avalon.law.yale.edu/18th_century/declare.asp. Additionally, there are few who understand that the element "pursuit of happiness" was taken from Locke's Second Treatise, and to Locke meant happiness, rights, and property. This is something seemingly negated in contemporary scholarship and discourse.

[85] Revert to Bailyn's statement on sovereignty in Chapter one.

of an absolute tyranny over these states.[86] (emphasis added)

These experiences and the history surrounding them are enumerated in the original declaration. In conjunction with the evidence from the previous chapters, it is known that sovereignty, legislative authority, and federalism was meant to hold constant for stability.[87] Out of 27 provisions in the Declaration of Independence only 8 are *not* directly related to sovereignty, legislative authority, and federalism.[88]

For sake of debate, it is reasonable to ascertain that this independence produced the ability to start anew. In other words, to encapsulate all of the previous experiences, debates, and theories into a solidified government. This was the Early American Republic's first attempt to establish their government unbeholden to the Crown. This first attempt, found in the Articles of Confederation, it should be known, is with the backdrop of real war in their own lands. This fact should not be construed liberally, or to be over or under exaggerated without cause. Speed was a necessity. With enemy troops literally marching through the fields, it is difficult to say the Articles were a "failure"[89]

---

[86] Declaration of Independence, July 4, 1776: http://avalon.law.yale.edu/18th_century/declare.asp.

[87] Representation is also within these known rationales. Revert to footnote 33 for reasoning on its neglect.

[88] Declaration of Independence, July 4, 1776: http://avalon.law.yale.edu/18th_century/declare.asp. Those 8 provisions are the "rights" of British Americans: trial by jury, quartering troops, unreasonable searches and seizures, taxation, petition, etc. Additionally, this means that on balance the weight of the objections were institutional (there were also interest objections in the sense of representation and the substance of the Sugar and Stamp Acts, but revert to foot note 88 and 33 for its neglect; also understand that those substantive acts were repealed and replaced with authoritarian mandates of capitulation).

[89] For example, many will respectfully charge that the Articles were clearly a failure because of all the self-interest and predatory economic tactics on other States, treaties with other nations, etc. All of these objections would be true, but it is also just as much a truism that shortly after British troops returned to England from the colonial's homes, businesses, inter alia there were rampant micro-economic issues with loyalists suing colonials for property rights of the businesses of the colonials that the loyalists took from the colonials during the war. See Henry Dawson, *The Case of Elizabeth Rutgers versus Joshua Waddington* (New York, 1866): https://archive.org/details/caseofelizabeth00rutg. Moreover, by the 1780s "Congress no longer enjoyed the confidence it had commanded in 1774 and 1775...when Madison presented his credentials on March 20, Congress was in the midst of overhauling its entire policy for sustaining the war"

(those that I know who assert this claim vitriolically have never faced real hardship let alone war). The ability to conceptualize the turmoil diminishes after time, unless reasserted and an attempt be made to re-analyze first principles.

The Articles of Confederation and Perpetual Union became the governing system of the new-found Early American Republic. It would appear, however, that the pendulum swung too far the other way. Instead of a centralized authoritarian regime with no *institutional* divisions, the framing generation of the Articles of Confederation made prudent governance for the whole at the general level almost impossible. The majority of the Articles of Confederation are negative rights, or powers, from the federal perspective. Meaning, save for Article IX that delineates the "right[s] and power[s]" of the federal government, the provisions were negatives on what the separate and individual States could *not* do: the compact was an agreement on what the State could not do as opposed to what the federal government could do.[90] Moreover, only few powers were delegated to the federal government but without enforcement clauses. On balance, the federal government did not have the ends for governing authority let alone the means of ensuring revenue being raised for the military. The individual States grew very strong on a very local scale. Eventually, this lack of counter balance to check the overt powerful States led to States engaging in predatory pricing, excess speculation, land trade and agreements to the west, and fabricating their own currencies in some cases,[91] which prompted discontent throughout the "league of friendship."[92] With

---

(see Rakove, *James Madison and the Creation of the American Republic*, 19).

[90] Benedict, *Sources in American Constitutional History*, 20-25.

[91] This is debatable notwithstanding popular opinion. Certainly, States like Rhode Island saw sever currency depreciation and inflation rates throughout the State. But in general, it would appear that most regional areas, within and without the separate States (trading and currency exchange were not exclusive to just that State for the most part, it crossed regional areas), relied more on the British pound and trading. Nevertheless, the lack of a strong unified currency proved difficult for the whole given the proximity of the separate and independent States.

[92] The intellectual elite were attempting to amend the Articles in order to govern the polity more efficiently. The issue, from their perspective, was the intense localism that Wood discussed. Madison, among others, was forthright in attempting to amend the Articles. The Annapolis Convention was called for this purpose, but only five States

the crushing weight of $200 million debt, Shay's Rebellion striking fear of the sword and of the electorate, and the other experiences led the Americans, again, to the need of divided authority federalism.[93]

The General Convention of 1787

This section is not an argument to prescribe the original intent for the whole of every provision of the Constitution.[94] Such a task is, while emphatically imperative for contemporary legal scholars, laborious and outside of the scope of this limited purpose of divided authority federalism. Original intent of the provisions and principles of the Constitution are taken from an amalgamation of sources: antecedents, the spectrum of debate, what the consequence of the debates were. What will be shown from this section and the next is the *general* original intent[95] of the framers with respect to federalism on the *institutional* principle. Additionally, and as a logical extension, laying the grounds to consider federalism an axiom, a law of nature. For as Alexander Hamilton states in *The Federalist no. 78*:

> *It can be no weight to say, that the courts on the pretence of a repugnancy, may substitute their own pleasure to the constitutional intentions of the legislature.* This might as well happen in the case of two contradictory statutes; or it might as well happen in every adjudication upon any single statute. *The courts must declare*

---

sent delegates. Under the Articles, virtually nothing could be done at the federal level without at least 9 of the 13 States in concurrence. The after math of Shay's Rebellion spurred the States to send delegates to a General Convention at Independence Hall in Philadelphia. Moreover, the majority of officials "accepted election to Congress reluctantly, aware that service in America's first national government meant absence from all the private concerns disrupted by the war" (see Rakove, *James Madison and the Creation of the American Republic*, 19).

[93] For an in-depth analysis of Shay's Rebellion see Stewart, *The Summer of 1787*, 11-16. For the $200 million debt that became too burdensome see Rakove, *James Madison and the Creation of the American Republic*, 19-29.

[94] To find these analyses in grave detail research any of the works done by Judge McConnell and Easterbrook, along with professors Barnett, McGuinnis, and Baude.

[95] To create doctrines for constitutional law would require volumes on each provision. This is the commencing of finding the original intent for federalism.

> *the sense of the law; and if they should be disposed to ex-*
> *ercise their WILL instead of JUDGEMENT, the conse-*
> *quence would equally be the substitution of their pleasure*
> *to that of the legislative body…If then the courts of justice*
> *are to be considered as the bulwarks of a limited constitu-*
> *tion against legislative encroachments,* this considera-
> tion will afford a strong argument for the permanent
> tenure of judicial offices, since nothing will con-
> tribute so much as this to that independent spirit of
> the judges.[96] (emphasis added)

George Washington, President of the Convention, would later state in his Farewell Address that the Constitution "until changed by an *explicit and authentic act of the whole people,* is sacredly *obligatory on all.*"[97] Thus, the point of understanding the original intent of the governing and fundamental law is not one to be discarded by simple objections and ought to be inquired with vigor. The proceeding sections move to understanding the concept of federalism and specifically *our* federalism (by our I mean mankind).

On Friday the 25th of May in 1787 quorum was reached in Independence Hall during the General Convention.[98] A few days later, Edmund Randolph proposed the Virginia Plan. The first provision articulates the purposes of the Convention:

> Resolved, that the articles of the confederation
> ought to be so corrected and enlarged as to accom-
> plish the objects proposed by their institution,
> namely, common defence, security of liberty, and
> general welfare.[99]

---

[96] Madison, Hamilton, Jay, *The Federalist Papers* (New York: Bantam Classics, 1982), 476.

[97] "Washington's Farewell Address 1796": http://avalon.law.yale.edu/18th_century/washing.asp.

[98] James Madison, translated by Adrienne Koch, *Notes of Debates in the Federal Convention of 1787* (New York and London: W.W. Norton & Company, 1987), 23.

[99] *Notes of the Secret Debates of the Federal Convention of 1787,* Taken by the Late Hon Robert Yates, Delegate State of New York: http://avalon.law.yale.edu/18th_century/yates.asp.

Prior to the Virginia Plan being proposed Randolph framed the purpose of revising the Articles. Randolph suggested that the delegates ought to enquire "1. into the properties, which such a government ought to possess, 2. the defects of the confederation, 3. the danger of our situation & 4. the remedy."[100] The Virginia Plan that Randolph proposed is recorded as the brainchild of James Madison. The young delegate Madison studied vigorously in the months leading to the Convention on the nature of confederations and attempted to discover why they failed. As Willliam Pierce said, "[Madison was] the best informed Man of any point in debate."[101]

Madison studied the ancient and modern confederacies sometime between April and June of 1786 in detail to try to provide an ailment to the deficiencies of the Articles. Madison found, in general, that confederations normally "tended toward *dissolution* or *impotency*."[102] *Dissolution* as seen in the Union of Crowns and the colonial relationship with the King-in-Parliament, and *impotency* as in the Articles of Confederation with drastic disparate State-federal relationship. Madison, the younger generation of experienced American statesman, saw that "[complete] individual independence of the States is utterly irreconcilable with their *aggregate sovereignty*."[103] While Madison found there to be too much multiplicity at the State level he still was calling for multiplicity. Madison was calling for principles of divided authority federalism with vertical and horizontal powers and checks, which ought to be "well organized and balanced."[104] The younger generation of American statesman now was on the contraposition of what

---

[100] Koch, *Notes of the Debates in the Federal Convention of 1787*, 28-29.

[101] Max Farrand, *Records of the Federal Convention, III*, 94.

[102] "Notes on Ancient and Modern Confederacies": https://founders.archives.gov/documents/Madison/01-09-02-0001.

[103] "From James Madison to George Washington, 16 April 1787": https://founders.archives.gov/documents/Madison/01-09-02-0208. Meaning that compact, even in its weakest form, cannot exist without some governing body with some sphere of power over the whole of compact. The pendulum was stuck to the other extreme.

[104] *Ibid.* Here is where it seems that contemporary scholars misunderstand Madison and the government he more or less framed as being of nationalist persuasion. It will not be until the ratification debates and many dissenting opinions that Madison elaborates on the national and federal characteristics in the general government. Most weight being on federal.

their older colleagues were in with England. Madison and later Hamilton sought the need for divided authority federalism, but from the tumult that it wrought for the general government because of the States: lack of vertical *institutional* division.

The Virginia Plan explicitly shows eight provisions with respect to the concept of divided authority federalism. The third resolution states "that the National legislature ought to consist of two branches." This shows a horizontal institutional division of authority. As one of the delegates opined "he had opposed the grant of powers to cong[ress] heretofore, because the whole power was vested in one body. The proposed distribution of the powers into different bodies changed the case."[105] One branch was intended to check upon the other. The fourth resolution reads, "the members of *the first branch of the National Legislature ought to be elected by the people of the several States*...to be ineligible to any office established by a particular State, or under the authority of the United States, except those peculiarly belonging to the functions of the first branch." This shows the *interests* division, that Gary Wills articulates, in "the people's chamber." The fifth resolution correlates with the fourth in that the upper chamber "*ought to be elected by those of the first, out of a proper number of persons nominated by the individual Legislatures*...and to be ineligible to any office established by a particular State, or under the authority of the United States, except those peculiarly belonging to the functions of the second branch." The intention here was to have "the people's" branch have some indirect effect on the upper chamber through their representatives' appointments. It also follows that the upper house was intended to be removed from the *interests* and is, therefore, more *institutional* with respect to the Virginia Plan.

The fourth and fifth provisions also show vertical institutional divisions in the sense that the members of the Congress could not hold dual positions in the State government. Then the ninth provision went back to a horizontal institutional division. The resolution declared "that a National Judiciary be established to consist of one or more supreme tribunals, and of inferior tribunals to be chosen by the

---

[105] Koch, *Notes of Debates in the Federal Convention of 1787*, 34.

National Legislature, to hold their offices during good behavior." [106]
Again, the intent was divide lawmaking power from the power of adjudication. The remainder of the debates this Wednesday May 30 of
1787 were more on terminology—an important point to be made on
linguistic accuracy—of federal versus national government, the States
in general, and briefly sovereignty.

Charles Pinckney, delegate of South Carolina, "wished to know
of Mr. Randolph whether he meant to abolish the States altogether"
given the language of the first resolution. Randolph responded that
"he meant by these general propositions merely to introduce the particular ones which explained the outlines of the system he had in
view."[107] The inferences to be drawn from the first government plan
proposed is that there was a call for a more qualitative mixed, divided
authority federalism.

Spirited debates on the provisions and purposes for the Convention with the backdrop of the Virginia Plan ensued for days. Most of
the contentions amongst the delegates—especially between the Large
and Small State blocs—dealt with the Virginia Plan, sovereignty, and
dividing authority. In respect to the mode of electing the executive,
George Mason on June 2 "opposed decidedly the making [of] the Executive the mere creature of the Legislature as a violation of the *fundamental principle of good Government.*" Madison and James Wilson
"both thought it *bad policy to introduce such a mixture* of the State authorities, where their agency could be otherwise supplied." John
Dickinson believed the concept of divided authority federalism to be
so important that "no man ought to be silent or reserved." Dickinson
went on in length about divided authority federalism:

> The Legislative, Executive, & Judiciary departments
> *ought to be made as independent as possible*; but that

---

[106] Koch, *Notes of the Debates of the Federal Convention of 1787*, 30-33. The other 8 provisions deal with Amendments and what is popularly known as Madison's Federal Negative, which was the source of contentious debate.

[107] Koch, *Notes of the Debates in the Federal Convention*, 34. These terms are important to understanding federalism, but this point will be analyzed in the next section entitled Ratification, The Federalists, and the Anti-Federalists.

such an Executive as some seemed to have in contemplation was not consistent with a republic: that a firm Executive could only exist in a limited monarchy. In the British Gov[ernment] itself the weight of the Executive arises from the attachments which the Crown draws to itself...*One source of stability [in the proposal] is the double branch of the Legislature. The division of the Country into distinct States formed the other principle source of stability.* This division ought therefore to be maintained, and considerable powers left to the States...*without this, and in case of consolidation of the States into one great Republic, we might read its fate in the history of smaller ones.*[108] (emphasis added)

Thus, despite the myriad opinions, arguments, votes, and re-votes that took place it is evident that divided authority federalism and by association multiple sovereignties was entrenched in the Convention and unequivocally dominated the substance of the proceedings.

The sixth resolution of the Virginia Plan, and Madison's own creation from his studies, was a touchy subject in the debate. This resolution proposed what is now known as Madison's Federal Negative.[109] On June 8, the delegates debated in length and voted down not to be remerged, save for private correspondence with Jefferson, the federal negative. As LaCroix suggests, "the debate surrounding James Madison's proposal to give Congress the power to negative state laws required delegates to work through the meaning of multiplicity."[110]

---

[108] Koch, *Notes of the Debates in the Federal Convention of 1787*, 56.

[109] Alison LaCroix, "The Authority for Federalism: Madison's Negative and the Origins of Federal Ideology," 28 Law and History Review 451 (2010).

[110] *Ibid*, 458. LaCroix attempts to argue that "the rejection of the negative and the adoption instead of a judicialized approach...signaled a fundamental shift" in federalism. In *The Ideological Origins of American Federalism* she argues that "following the demise of the federal negative, with its legislative solution to the problem of establishing a hierarchy of authorities, the delegates began to consider seriously the possibility of a judicial approach" (p. 161). Other scholars have held the same position with the supremacy clause. That it "must therefore be seen as following from, and causally related to, the defeat of the negative" (p. 162). The rationale is that the supremacy clause first appears in the New Jersey Plan, the opposition to the Virginia Plan, and suggesting the State

Pinckney commenced the deliberations by "mov[ing] that the National Legislature sh[ould] have authority to negative all laws which they sh[ould] judge to be improper." This proposal was the Federal Negative provision, which quickly reminded the delegates of the Declaratory Act. Madison quickly seconded and found that "the negative was the mildest expedient that could be devised for preventing mischiefs." That this vertical institutional check would "prevent attempts to commit them."[111] The next delegate, "Mr. Williamson was ag[ainst] giving a power that might restrain the States from regulating their internal police." Elbridge Gerry was against all arbitrary powers and did "not see the extent of such a power."[112] Gerry provided a robust analysis of divided authority federalism and the effects of such a negative:

> The proposed negative would extend to the regulations of the Militia, a matter on which the existence of a State might depend. The National Legislature with such a power may enslave the States. Such an idea as this will never be acceded to. It has never been suggested or conceived among the people... *The States too have different interests and are ignorant of each other's interests. The negative will therefore be abused.*[113] (emphasis added)

Roger Sherman requested for a possible enumeration of the cases as opposed to the echoing of the Declaratory Act. James Wilson found any attempt to define such cases would be impracticable:

> Abuses of the power over the individual person may happen as well as over the individual States. Federal

---

courts would therefore be bound. Of the framers, none explicitly said this. And even of the founder's only Jefferson is the only one who suggested it in a response letter from France to James Madison on June 20, 1787. Thus, it is not reasonably to ascertain this as being the intent without more.

[111] Koch, *Notes of the Debates in the Federal Convention of 1787*, 88.

[112] Koch, *Notes of the Debates in the Federal Convention of 1787*, 89.

[113] *Ibid*, 90.

liberty is to States, what civil liberty, is to private individuals. And States are not more unwilling to purchase it, by the necessary concession of their
political sovereignty, that the savage is to purchase
civil liberty by the surrender of his personal sovereignty, which he enjoys in a State of Nature. A definition of the cases in which the Negative should be
exercised, is impracticable....Among the first sentiments expressed in the first Congress was that Virginia is no more, that Massachusetts is no more...
We are now one nation of brethren.[114]

As is shown, Wilson not only viewed the enumeration as irrelevant
but also desired the States to limit their sovereignty enough to have
a functioning compact. Moreover, there is a trend to use this statement to justify an *opinion* that States did not retain sovereignty. This,
as will be shown momentarily, is conjecture and a delusional claim of
some of contemporary society.

Dickinson, next, contended that enumeration was also impossible
and since the States' power drastically overshadowed the federal governments, then if the negative was accepted some line had to be
drawn. Gunning Bedford found the negative would "strip the small
states of their equal suffrage."[115]

The barrage of positions illuminate the strength of divided authority federalism; the natural formative power. Sovereignty and division of powers from the vertical institutional perspective was the
forefront of discussion. This suggests not only the raw power of divided authority federalism, but more importantly the fine tuned tensions and weeding out of the best governance structures through
intense deliberations from all corners of the polity. Whereas this was
the only day for debate on the negative, the deliberations over sovereignty and divided authority federalism grew longer and deeper—de-
ducing as far as the intellectual elite's minds could go. Eventually, the

---

[114] *Ibid.*

[115] Koch, *Notes of the Debates in the Federal Convention of 1787*, 91.

New Jersey Plan was proposed and it resembled more of the Articles with only the additions of certain topics viewed as pressing and of the federal government's persuasion.

On June 15, William Patterson "laid before the Convention the plan which he said several of the deputations wished to be substituted in place of that proposed by Mr. Randolph."[116] The first resolution, in contrast with the Virginia Plan, reads:

> Res[olved] that the articles of Confederation ought to be so revised, corrected & enlarged, as to render the federal Constitution adequate to the exigencies of Government, & the preservation of the Union.[117]

The provisions of the New Jersey Plan were "addition[s] to the powers vested in the U[nited] States Congress."[118] Such powers included raising revenue, levying duties, regulation of trade and commerce, inter alia. The delegates proceeded to argue in length on the two plans, sovereignty, and divided authority federalism. Again, these delegates continued to fine tune their understandings.

Perhaps the most substantive debate came on June 21 when the delegates voted on the bicameral legislature provision. Doctor Johnson gave a brief analysis of the dominating issues between the two proposals:

> On comparison of the two plans which had been proposed from Virginia & N. Jersey, it appeared that the peculiarity which characterized the latter was being calculated to preserve the individuality of the States. The plan from Virginia did not profess to destroy this individuality altogether, but was charged with such tendency...they wished to leave the States in possession of considerable, tho'

---

[116] *Ibid*, 118.

[117] Koch, *Notes of the Debates in the Federal Convention of 1787*, 118.

[118] *Ibid*.

a subordinate jurisdiction. They had not yet however shewn how this could consist with, or be secured
against the general sovereignty & jurisdiction, which
they proposed to give to the national government. If
this could be shewn in such a manner as to satisfy the
patrons of the N. Jersey propositions, that the indi-
viduality of the States would not be endangered, many
of their objections would no doubt be removed.[119]

Wilson, out of the great respect for Doctor Johnson, ascertained that
"jealousy & rivalship would be felt between the General & particular
governments."[120] Moreover, there would be no intrusion from the
federal government unto the States because they were the more inti-
mate of the people over an extended republic. Given that Wilson did
not really address Doctor Johnson's points Madison weighed in. To
Madison, there was "less danger of encroachment from the General
Government than from the State Government."[121] That confederacies
tended more towards anarchy than tyranny: disobedience of the people than of usurpation.

The back and forth deliberations persisted all summer in 1787;
becoming more nuanced, liberal in uses, and exhaustive. The framer's
were carving out the divided authority federalism found within the
text and spirit of the Constitution. A consequence of which manifested
divided authority federalism in the institutions, rights, and *enumerated*
powers thereof, with vertical and horizontal institutional divisions.

Ratification, The Federalists, and The Anti-Federalists
From the outset a very important note is needed for context. "The people" in the context of 1787 was roughly ten percent of the actual pop-
ulation (or so I kept hearing in lectures, though they cannot be
recorded). Of that ten percent there is the dichotomy of the proto-elite
and the intellectual elites. There is a constant attempt to delegitimize

---

[119] Koch, *Notes of the Debates in the Federal Convention of 1787*, 163.

[120] *Ibid*, 164.

[121] *Ibid*, 164-165.

the *Federalist Papers* because its supporters engaged, correctly asserted, in chicanery to attain ratification of the Constitution throughout the ratification period (see the Federalists in the Pennsylvania Ratification proceedings). But to what status of people? This book, however, is not an evaluation of rather or not the Anti-Federalist's arguments were not given enough time to be reviewed. This is a qualitative and intellectually deep analysis of federalism and more importantly divided authority federalism as a law of nature. To ascertain that the lack of widespread publication has a significant impact on the outcome is illusory with the reality of "the people" and the publication distribution that the Anti-Federalist arguments did receive. Moreover, many of the sporadic arguments were regurgitated over again in the actual ratification conventions and in the *Anti-Federalists* which the *Federalists* addressed relentlessly. Thus, regardless of Madison's statements in Congress in 1796 about "as the instrument came from them, it was nothing more than the draught of a plan, nothing but a dead letter, until life and validity were breathed into it, by the voice of the people," scrutiny brings to light that this statement is more about the act of voting aye to ratification. And of the people who argued the anti-federalist positions, the objections were responded to exhaustively.

The intellectual elite at the Convention sent the Constitution to the Continental Congress to be disseminated, discussed, and either ratified or not to the proto-elite in the States. As Pauline Maier articulates, "two days after the Convention adjourned, six Philadelphia newspapers had printed the Constitution." By the end of 1787 "as many as two hundred" copies were printed.[122] The newspapers and pamphlets were the modes of communication outside of the actual proceedings.[123] On October 6, the great debate and first defense of

---

[122] Pauline Maier, *Ratification* (New York: Simon & Schuster, 2010), 70.

[123] *Ibid.* Maier contends that "by the late 1780s, the United States had about ninety-five newspapers, over twice the number at the time of independence." Moreover, and perhaps the most strikingly interesting, she goes on to say "there even a few that appeared daily to satisfy the hungry reading public." Whereas there was not a utopian egalitarian press with respect to the discourse of the ratification era; it is still clear that the Anti-Federalists had the time and ability to present their objections. Now, whether there was a chilling effect, as was the case in Pennsylvania, across the extended republic

the Constitution commenced with a speech in the Pennsylvania assembly by James Wilson.

In Pennsylvania, at the time of the ratification debates, the "legislature was in session when the new Constitution was referred to the states."[124] The legislature asked Wilson to explain the Constitution and answer inquiries and challenges levied.[125] As Wilson states, his purpose was to "lay...any information which will serve to explain and elucidate *the principles and arrangements* of the constitution."[126] In so doing, Wilson's first substantive remarks read:

> When the people established the powers of legislation under their separate governments, they invested their representatives with *every right and authority which they did not in explicit terms reserve*; and therefore upon every question respecting the jurisdiction of the House of Assembly, if the frame of government is silent, the jurisdiction is efficient and complete. *But in delegating federal powers*, another criterion was necessarily introduced, and *the congressional power is to be collected, not from tacit implication, but from the positive grant expressed* in the instrument

---

is well documented debate. For example, the first published criticism of the Constitution was rather mild, but it provoked a fierce response in the Independent Gazetteer with threats of "TAR and FEATHERS." "Fair Play answered the threats leveled against those who criticized the Constitution by insisting 'that the LIBERTY OF THE PRESS—the great bulwark of all the liberties of the people—ought never be restrained." Thus, it is fact that there were some outlets that were free and disseminated pamphlets throughout the ratification. The Philadelphia's Freeman's Journal slogan stated: OPEN TO ALL PARTIES, BUT INFLUENCED BY NONE (see pages 70-95). If there is any reasoned point that somehow all of this—or any other social norm or event—negates the wisdom of divided authority federalism, I would be open to reading an ambitious analysis.

[124] *The Anti-Federalist Papers and the Constitutional Convention Debates*, edited by Ralph Ketcham (New York: Signent Classic, 1986), 183.

[125] *Ibid.*

[126] *The Documentary History of the Ratification of the Constitution: Volume II, Pennsylvania*, edited by Merril Jensen (Wisconsin: The State Historical Society of Wisconsin, 1976), 167-172.

of union. Hence, it is evident, that in *the former case everything which is not reserved is given; but in the latter the reverse of the proposition prevails, and everything which is not given is reserved.*[127] (emphasis added)

Recall that federalism is divided authority, which was viewed by the English and loyalists as a solecism. Here, it may be said, is one of the first points one can see the argument against the notion of the framer's creating a solecism: divisions in enumerated rights and powers; supreme within certain spheres.

Wilson, then, addressing fear of rights being oppressed by the new federal government felt the objections unfounded. In rhetorical response Wilson stated, "nay, that very declaration might have been construed to imply that some degree of power was given, *since we undertook to define its extent.*"[128] Proceeding on to state-federal relationships Wilson felt it necessary to provide the contextual purpose of the Convention:

> Let it be remembered then, that the business of the Federal Convention was not local, but general—not limited to the views and establishments of a single State, but co-extensive with the continent, and comprehending the views and establishments of *thirteen independent sovereignties.*[129] (emphasis added)

---

[127] *Ibid.* Unfortunately contemporary times makes it apparent that I need to re-state "everything which is not given is reserved."

[128] *The Documentary History of the Ratification of the Constitution*, edited by Merril Jensen, 167-172.

[129] *Ibid.* This is a piece of evidence that has long be negated from federalism scholarship. There has been a consistent trend to only revert to Wilson's remarks at the Convention when he said, "when the Colonies became independent of G. Britian, they became independent also of each other. He read the declaration of independence, observing thereon that the United Colonies were declared to be free & independent States; and inferring that they were independent, not *Individually* but *Unitedly*." Since 1907 there has been a dichotomy in federalism scholarship on the point of sovereignty. Either the States were sovereign or they were not. The evidence I keep providing shows that the group that accedes the latter are folly. See Claude Van Tyne, "Sovereignty in the American Revolution: A Historical Study," 12 Am. Hist. Rev. 529 (1907); Charles Lofgren, "The Origins of the Tenth Amendment: History, Sovereignty, and

Then he addressed the Anti-Federalists objections as to the "baneful aristocracy"—what would later be echoed on the national scale in *The Anti-Federalist* paper *Centinel I*—of the federal Senate. To this effect, Wilson held:

> Perhaps there never was a charge made with less reasons than that which predicts the institution of a baneful aristocracy in the federal Senate. This body branches into two characters, the one legislative and the other executive. In its legislative character it can effect no purpose, without the co-operation of the House of Representatives, and in its executive character it can accomplish no object without the concurrence of the President. Thus fettered, I do not know any act which the Senate can of itself perform, and such dependency necessarily precludes every idea of influence and superiority.[130]

Recall that federalism is divided authority. Wilson would continue a robust rebuttal to the objections of the structure of Article I of the Constitution. All of the arguments and points of dissection of the Constitution's meaning are premised on divided authority federalism. The other inferences to be drawn are that the Anti-Federalists were deeply worried about consolidated authority. So, the principled objections, save for a few, were about fears of undivided authority.

In Virginia, the same objections were raised in the "most moving, eloquent denial by the anti-federalists of the need for a more energetic

---

the Problem of Constitutional Intention," in Constitutional Government in America, 331 (R. Collins ed. 1981); Richard Morris, "We the People of the United States: The Bicentennial of a People's Revolution," 82 Am. Hist. Rev. I (1977); Edward Corwin, "The Passing of Dual Federalism," 36 Va. L. Rev. I, 3 (1950); Richard Posner, "Toward an Economic Theory of Federal Jurisdiction," in Symposium on Federalism, 6 Harv. J. of Law & Public Policy 41 (1982); The Federalist Society's 2012 National Lawyers Convention, in symposium on Federalism and Federal Powers (Nov., 2012).

[130] *The Documentary History of the Ratification of the Constitution*, edited by Merril Jensen, 167-172.

government."[131] That moving and eloquent speech came on June 5th and 7th from Patrick Henry. Henry's opening remarks are thusly:

> The fate of this question and America may depend
> on this: Have they said, we the States? Have they
> made a proposal of a compact between States? If
> they had, this would be a confederation: It is other-
> wise most clearly a consolidated government. The
> question turns, Sir, on that poor little thing—the ex-
> pression, We, the people, instead of the States of
> America. I need not take much pains to show, that
> the principles of this system, are extremely perni-
> cious, impolitic, and dangerous. Is this Monarchy,
> like England—a compact between Prince and peo-
> ple; with checks on the former, to secure the liberty
> of the latter? is this a confederacy, like Holland—an
> association of a number of independent States, each
> of which retain its individual sovereignty?[132]

Again, the entire spectrum shows an intrinsic desire for divided authority federalism (Fun Fact: In Mary Builders *Madison's Hand* she
shows how the original transcript was supposed to read "We the
States." Further hitting at the natural division and contention with
respect to first principles). Henry continues the vein of State-federal
relations and sovereignty on June 5th and then reconvened on June
7th. The totality of the Brutus papers show that the majority of the
objections were premised on consolidated powers.[133] John Jay, James
Madison, and Alexander Hamilton responded to every point in grave
detail with citations of authority, relentless reason, and experience in
The Federalist under the moniker 'Publius.'

One of those citations of authority was the revered Montesquieu.
As figures 1 and 3 show, the works of Montesquieu were the most

---

[131] *The Anti-Federalist Papers*, edited by Ralph Ketcham, forward to speech p. 199.

[132] *The Anti-Federalist Papers*, edited by Ralph Ketcham, 199-216.

[133] *Ibid*, 269-310.

cited. Montesquieu in his *Spirit of the Laws* discusses in length the necessity for a stable polity to divide authority. Additionally, both *The Federalist* and *The Anti-Federalist* learned from a variety of sources of thought and high quality of sources within the intellectual elite as figures 2 and 3 show below.

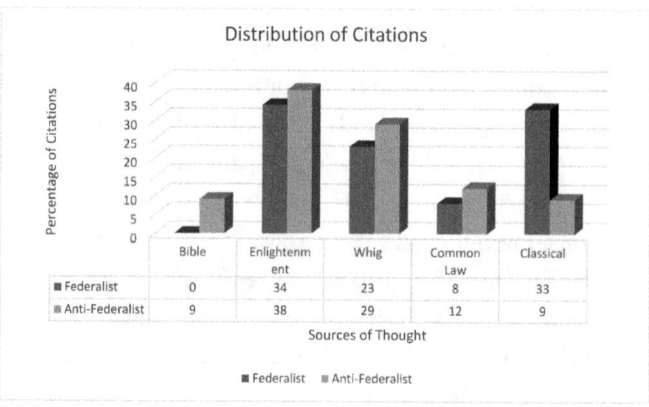

Figure 2. Distribution of Citations By Sources of Thought

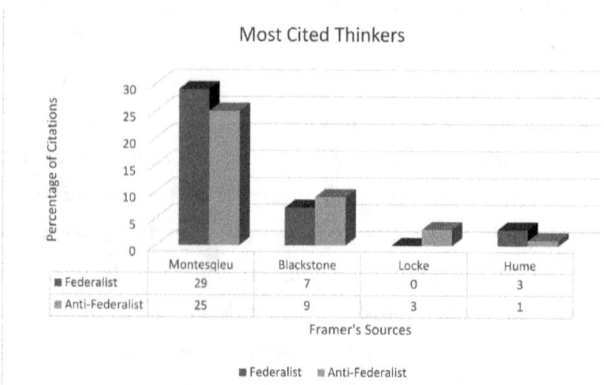

Figure 3. Most Cited Thinkers Broken Down By Group

Both sides during the ratification debates came from prestigious families and received elite educations. Relying on their education and experiences *The Federalist* addressed, inter alia, the three dominate points:

form of government created, the source of the government, and sovereignty. All of which are premised on divided authority federalism.

The Federalist no. 39[134] executes the analysis of the form of government created by the delegates of the Convention. It begins, logically, with the first necessary point of inquiry and then analyzes:

> The first question that offers itself is, whether the general form and aspect of government be strictly republican? It is evident that no other form would be reconcileable with the genius of the people of America; with the fundamental principles of the revolution; or with that honorable determination, which animates every votary of freedom, to rest all our political experiments on the capacity of mankind for self-government. If the plan of the Convention therefor be found to depart from the republican character, its advocates must abandon it as no longer defensible.[135]

But what does this even mean? Are there not myriad variances of the theory of republican government? To clarify *Federalist no. 39* reads:

> If we resort for a criterion, to the different principles on which different forms of government are established, we may define a republic to be, or at least may bestow that name on, a government which derives all its powers directly or indirectly from the great body of the people…on comparing the Constitution planned by the Convention, with the standard here fixed, we perceive at once that it is in the most rigid sense conformable to it. The House of

---

[134] Because of pragmatic limitations I will only use no. 39. This should not be misconstrued as being the only paper that addresses divided authority federalism. This thesis proves that and to go beyond this point is to kick the can down the road.

[135] *The Federalist Papers*, edited by Gary Wills, 227.

Representatives, like that of one branch at least of all the Stat Legislatures, is elected immediately by the great body of the people. The Senate, like the present Congress, and the Senate of Maryland, derives its appointment indirectly from the people. The President is indirectly derived from the choice of the people.[136]

The objections of the Anti-Federalists were known though; and, moreover, many of the arguments hashed out in the Convention on terminology. Nevertheless, Federalist no. 39 addresses the objections again:

But it was not sufficient, say the adversaries of the proposed Constitution, for the Convention to adhere to the republican form. They ought, with equal care, to have preserved the *federal* form, which regards the union as a *confederacy* of sovereign States; instead of which, they have framed a *national* government, which regards the union as a *consolidation* of the States.[137] (emphasis added)

Echoing themselves in *Federalists no. 9* and *10*, they go on to explain the form of government. "On examining the first relation," they wrote, "it appears on one hand that the Constitution is to be founded on the assent and ratification of the people...[through the] deputies elected for the special purpose." Moreover, "it is to be the assent and ratification of the several States, derived from the supreme authority in each State...the people."[138] That "each State" with providing their consent of ratification "is considered as a *sovereign body* independent of all others." Thus, the mode of legitimacy for the Constitution was a *federal* act and not national. Meaning, the

---

[136] *Ibid*, 228-229.

[137] *The Federalist Papers*, edited by Gary Wills, 230.

[138] *Ibid*.

sovereign body resides in the people distributed across the extended republic via the States thereof.

In respect to the operation of powers it is a *national* form in that it is controlling on the people in their individual capacities. Notwithstanding, "if the government be national with regard to the *operation* of its powers *(policies affect every individual equally)*, it changes its aspect again when we contemplate it in relation to the *extent* of its powers."[139] As the aforementioned evidences the ingenuity of the framers established a divided authority federalism system.

The Federalists, along with the totality of the data, show divided authority federalism was the intent of the Constitution. What was objected and answered; what was re-objected and re-answered as to the form of government created is forthrightly addressed:

> The idea of a national Government involves in it, not only an authority over the individual citizens; but an indefinite supremacy over all persons and things, so far as they are objects of lawful Government... Among communities united for particular purposes, it is vested partly in the general, and partly in the municipal legislatures...In the latter the local or municipal authorities form distinct and independent portions of the supremacy, no more subject within their respected spheres to the general authority, than the general authority is subject to them, within its own sphere. In this relation then the proposed Government cannot be deemed a national one; since its jurisdiction extends to certain enumerated objects only, and leaves to the several States a residuary and inviolable sovereignty over all other objects.[140]

Federalism as properly defined: multiplicity of polities, with different interests, collected under one compact, over an extended republic,

---

[139] *Ibid*, 232.

[140] *The Federalist Papers*, edited by Gary Wills, 232-233.

with institutional divisions within respected spheres of sovereignty. As this book has attempted to prove; federalism is divided authority and was the unwitting intent of the collected minds of the Early American Republic.

CHAPTER IV —

Logic and Uncertainty in a Post-Modernist World

We, in this country, must be willing to do battle for
old ideas that have proved their value with the same
enthusiasm that people do for new ideas and creeds.
—John F. Kennedy,
congressional campaign speech, 1946

We, as one common people, originating from the same Creator, or
originating from the same methodical accumulation of atoms, are in
interesting but not at all unfamiliar times (see every progressive era,
fight between capitalism vs. communism, and disregard for truth). Irrespective of the political ideological origins there is frenzy and mass
hysteria pretty much anywhere you go. In fact, the readers that cur-
tailed their biases to reach this point are probably in agreement with
that vague statement even though if we discussed the substance of it
we would disagree widely. As it should be, because you will never find
a Utopia of thought or life in this world. Just a series of paradoxes
with better explanations than others. So, how do we heal and grow as
mostly all people attempt to do?

I thought that after the Election of 2016 there would be a show-
ing of humility throughout the extended republic and the world (because to pretend the populist revolt, or any period, is purely within
the American polity is erroneous). I surely thought this would be the
case for the, supposedly, most enlightened institution: the academy.
Thousands of years of history, theology, and science has led to many
conclusions. Some withstanding the test of time, and others proven
antithetical to absolute truth. So much knowledge discovered and yet
we cannot simply grasp the idea that one cannot provide sources on

what has not been studied. So many rhetorical opinions and yet we cannot simply grasp that not all opinions have empirical backdrops; but that does not simply invalidate that individual's opinion (like contemporary abortion debates). The simple concept of truth is so complex that the vast majority of us all have no idea of its complexity.[141] No idea that in can be true that X occurred, but just as true that X could have been negated by Y in that circumstance. Or, that it is true that X, Y, and Z supports claim A, but also just as true that e1, e2, and e3 supports the contraposition of claim A (insert just about anything on the mass media). Yet, we still act primitively when faced with evidence or opinions that does not conform to preconceived conclusions. Even this logic is used as a weapon against those that oppose our own preconceived conclusions. This, undoubtedly, comes from our hive mentality that evolutionary psychology has described.[142] Just now, my little sister said, "are you playing stuff?" I responded, "no." She countered, "yes you are and it's from that device." And walked away. Irrespective of the falsehood that one of my electronic devices was playing music; something as trivial as this hit the evolutionary wall of our minds.

Individuals of all creeds and educational attainment ought never to pretend they have *all* the answers. This maladaptive thought breeds a cynical world. Imagine a world where everyone only believed they were correct and everyone else folly. Imagine that world being governed, and intellectual conclusions derived the same way. How would anything be resolved or even objective? Given that with increased diversity comes increased conflict is it not salient to ensure we first move to understanding each other, thinking with logical foundations, and being civil in discourse? There will never be agreement but there can always be civil disagreement in hopes of finding the next least worst explanation. Nevertheless, the chicken-or-egg paradox will persist. Therefore, one ultimate answer will never be found. So, with this as

---

[141] Glanzberg, Michael, "Truth", The Stanford Encyclopedia of Philosophy (Winter 2016 Edition), Edward N. Zalta (ed.), URL = https://plato.stanford.edu/archives/win2016/entries/truth/.

[142] Haidt, Jonathan. The Righteous Mind: Why Good People are Divided by Politics and Religion. S.l.: Penguin Books Ltd, 2013.

a truth (open to counters), then what should be the most protected concepts of our societies? Probably those truths, the laws of nature, that came from old wisdom and have been confirmed repeatedly throughout time (like gravity and multicultural identity), should be the most protected concepts of our societies.

One of those laws, I hold, is the concept of divided authority federalism with a general sovereign that creates a baseline for societal norms, laws, and policies. Much like the US Constitution establishes a baseline for individual rights not to be usurped by the government, but does not dictate individuals day-to-day lives. In contemporary times the American system has seen a gross negligence in the general government with respect to federalism (when the President can walk into Congress and say he, or she, makes the law there is a fundamental issue). Executive orders and policy memos effectively circumventing congress (my liberal friends can now appreciate the severity of "conservative intelligence" on this issue through the Obama era, because someone they think is deplorable is in office). The Judiciary legislating from the bench whether conservative or liberal interpretation as opposed to trying to find the original understanding (my conservative friends can now appreciate this with the previous decades of liberal interpretation on the Court). Why is it so impossible to disassociate what the law says from the policy outcome on a mass scale? Why is it so impossible to go "okay, thank you Supreme Court for the ruling on the constitutionality of the issue. We do not like it, we will change it through the amendment process." Maybe the issue comes from the exact reason the first principles were instantiated into the Constitution: we prefer not to be controlled by a tyrannical minority or majority voice. Maybe it's the biases in civil education and academia in general?[143] Much like the issues with Gerrymandering and Duverger's Law. Much like the Us vs. Them mentality that I found infecting the academy in my discipline and drove me to pursue other ends (Comedy Central is not acceptable during class time by any professor).

---

[143] https://heterodoxacademy.org/index.php/the-problem/. Jonathan Haidt and roughly "1,700 professors and graduate students" bringing what once was "conservative hysteria" to light about academic biases unwittingly becoming an issue.

As a first-generation college student, I came from the bottom. Almost the very bottom. My mom, the sweetest woman in the world, worked for the mentally disabled making $9/hr trying to support 3 kids (my two older sisters and I). I recall never knowing if Christmas was going to be celebrated that year or not. I recall not knowing if we would have enough for food that week. I recall knowing we couldn't afford things like new cabinet doors after the termites dissolved the once frame. I also recalled the culture and self-segregation of my class of people. I recall everyone having different experiences, thoughts, and biases. Moreover, and most importantly, I recall how impossible it was for one to truly empathize what the others were going through. This is a culture that has a local centric view of things. And when I grew, went away for the army, came back and went to school, obtained a fellowship in DC, and analyzed the cultures of different people across the world; I found that it is the same everywhere just on different scales and playing different notes. So, what then?

The aforementioned is why federalism is imperative to stability across millennia, generations, and cultures of a polity whether a global, national, or State government. It is also why, inter alia, federalism is a law of nature. One that Prof. Horowitz and Oosthuizen discovered in African tribes across the continent a while ago and keep discovering.[144] A law that the American system has not adhered to for some time.[145] As Fischer and Devins explain:

> 1990's federalism decisions are also a testament to the power of elected government to shape the Court. Through judicial appointments, executive orders, the Contract with America, and the potent lobbying of state officials, the Supreme Court's revival of federalism is very much a product of its times. For this very reason, it is not surprising that the Rehnquist Court eventually limited the reach of its federalism

---

[144] Oosthuizen and Horowitz. Federalism in South Africa. Politikon, vol. 3, iss. 2, 1986.

[145] Fisher, Louis, and Neal Devins. Political dynamics of constitutional law. St. Paul, MN: Thomson/West, 2011.

revival. Rather than extend its 1990s rulings, the Justices backed away from those rulings in order to uphold politically popular bills...In so doing, the Court made clear that it would not risk political backlash by embracing federalism rulings that challenged the New Deal or Great Society reforms.[146]

Because instead of objectivity and clarity we prefer bias ideology? Have we seen first principles adhered to and logic control the day? Not when Supreme Court Justices speak out that Congress retains a "presumption of constitutionality" even though this has been stretched in practice to carte blanche.[147] I am curious as to what my philosophy friends think about presumptions and the logic of predetermined bias. I suspect the response would not be too kind or one in favor to not withstand scrutiny when pressed with opposition. For example, to my liberal friends I do not perceive a presumption of GOP correctness to go over well. Conversely, to my conservative friends I do not perceive a presumption of liberal correctness to go over well either. Seems to me like a neutral principle should be applied. Maybe Robert Bork was not such a radical? Of course, one cannot say that lest social ostracism.

As we enter, or are fully entrenched, in a post-modernist intellectual paradigm it is prudent to reflect on the literature, use logic to derive conclusions, try to steer the emotional elephant away from pure emotion, and still hold onto objective truth. For all the points of debate, new knowledge to be discovered, and even originalists dealing with indeterminacy[148] why are we diluted enough to think we do not have to adhere to the laws of nature that generations after generations have discovered through tumultuous times and mistakes (like the necessity for free speech)? Divided authority federalism, for the sake of a stable polity, must be viewed socially, politically, and

---

[146] *Ibid*, 77.

[147] *Ibid*, 84.

[148] Mannheimer, Michael. "The Contingent Fourth Amendment." SSRN Electronic Journal, 2013. doi:10.2139/ssrn.2366486.

legally as a law of nature and adhered to thusly. Disenfranchisement (for legal citizens), political partisanship (Us vs. Them mentalities), and negation of federalism as a fundamental law must end. But most importantly we must show humility and try to understand what contradicts our ideas.

BIBLIOGRAPHY

—Primary Sources

Charles Inglis, *The True Interest of America Impartially State, in Certain Strictures on a Pamphlet Intitled Common Sense*. Philadelphia: Humphreys, 1776.

Thomas Jefferson, *Writings*. New York: The Library of America, 1984.

John Adams, "Thoughts on Government," https://www.masshist.org/publications/apde2/view?&id=PJA04 dg2.

"John Adams to James Warren, April 20, 1776," https://www.masshist.org/publications/apde2/view?&id=PJA04 d062#ptrPJA04d062n3.

"John Adams autobiography, part 1, 'John Adams,' through 1776 sheet 23 of 53, January-April 1776," http://www.masshist.org/digitaladams/archive/doc?id=A1_23& bc=%2Fdigitaladams%2Farchive%2Fbrowse%2Fautobio1.php.

[John Trenchard and Thomas Gordon], *Cato's Letters, vol. 2*. London: W. Wilkins, T. Woodward, J. Walthoe, and J. Peele, 1723.

Letter from Thomas Jefferson to Thomas Mann Randolph, Jr., 30 May 1790: https://founders.archives.gov/documents/Jeffer-son/01-16-02-0264.

Thomas Hobbes, *Leviathan*. London: Penguin Books, 1985.

Sir William Blackstone, *Commentaries on the laws of England*. Chicago: Forgotten Books, 2012.

James Otis, *Rights of the British Colonies* (JHL 7).

Garry Wills, *The Federalist Papers*. New York: Bantam Book, 1982.

Art. I §1-2, United States Constitution, http://avalon.law.yale.edu/18th_century/art1.asp.

The Stamp Act, March 22, 1765:
http://avalon.law.yale.edu/18th_century/stamp_act_1765.asp.

"John Adams diary 11, 18-29 December 1765":
http://www.masshist.org/digitaladams/archive/doc?id=D11&nu mrecs=2&archive=all&hi=on&mode=&query=1765%2520WE DNESDAY&queryid=&rec=1&start=1&tag=text.

Declaration of Independence, July 4, 1776:
http://avalon.law.yale.edu/18th_century/declare.asp.

Henry Dawson, *The Case of Elizabeth Rutgers versus Joshua Wadding-ton* (New York, 1866): https://archive.org/details/caseofeliza-bethr00rutg.

"Washington's Farewell Address 1796":
http://avalon.law.yale.edu/18th_century/washing.asp.

James Madison, translated by Adrienne Koch, *Notes of Debates in the Federal Convention of 1787* (New York and London: W.W. Norton & Company, 1987), 23.

Notes of the Secret Debates of the Federal Convention of 1787, Taken by the Late Hon Robert Yates, Delegate State of New York: http://avalon.law.yale.edu/18th_century/yates.asp.

"Notes on Ancient and Modern Confederacies":
https://founders.archives.gov/documents/Madison/01-09-02-0001.

"From James Madison to George Washington, 16 April 1787":
https://founders.archives.gov/documents/Madison/01-09-02-0208.

The Anti-Federalist Papers, edited by Ralph Ketcham. New York: Signet Classic, 1986.

The Documentary History of the Ratification of the Constitution: Volume II, Pennsylvania, edited by Merril Jensen. Wisconsin: The State Historical Society of Wisconsin, 1976.

Sir Walter Bart, Tales of a Grandfather (Edinburgh: Constable Printer to Her Majesty), chapter XXXIII.

—Secondary Sources

Bernard Bailyn, *The Ideological Origins of the American Revolution.*

Cambridge, Massachusetts: The Belknap Press of Harvard University Press, 1967.

Pauline Maier, "A Pearl in a Gnarled Shell: Gordon S. Wood's The Creation of the American Republic Reconsidered," The William and Mary Quarterly Vol. 44, No. 3 (1987).

Marshall Smelser, "The Federalist Period as an Age of Passion," American Quarterly Vol. 10, No. 4 (1958).

Elkins and McKitrick, *The Age of Federalism*. New York & Oxford: Oxford University Press, 1993.

Gordon Wood, *The Creation of the American Republic 1776-1787*. University of North Carolina Press, 1969.

Alison LaCroix, *The Ideological Origins of American Federalism*. Cambridge, Massachusetts & London, England: Harvard University Press, 2010.

Christopher Collier and James Collier, *Decisions in Philadelphia: The Constitutional Convention of 1787*. New York: Ballantine Books, 2007.

Jack Rakove, *James Madison and the Creation of the American Republic*.

David Stewart, *The Summer of 1787*. New York: Simon & Schuster Paperbacks, 2007.

The Great Lecture Series, The mind of the enlightenment, cassette tapes of lectures by Alan Kors at the University of Pennsylvania, 1991.

Donald Lutz, "The Relative Influence of European Writers on Late Eighteenth-Century American Political Thought," The American Political Science Review, Vol. 78, No. 1 (1984): 189-197.

Cruz, Ted. "Clipping the Wings of Angels: The History and Theory behind the Ninth and Tenth Amendments of the United States Constitution." Undergraduate Thesis, Princeton University, 1992.

Berger, Federalism: The Founder's Design.

Robert Dahl, *How Democratic is the American Constitution?*. New Haven & London: Yale University Press, 2003.

Angerholzer III, et al., *Triumphs and Tragedies of the Modern Presidency: Case Studies in Presidential Leadership* (California and Colorado: Praeger, 2016), 192.

Michael Stolleis, *The Law Under the Swastika* (Chicago and London: The University of Chicago Press, 1998), 1-40, 48-102.

Benton and Ford, Rage for Order (Cambridge and London: Harvard University Press, 2016), 1-18, 28-55.

Gordon Wood, "Federalism from the Bottom Up," The University of Chicago Law Review 78 (2011): 706.

Magnus Magnusson, *Scotland: The Story of a Nation*. New York: Grove Press, 2000.

Brian Levack, *The Formation of the British State: England , Scotland, and the Union, 1603-1707*. Oxford: Clarendon Press, 1987.

Michael Benedict, *Sources in American Constitutional History*. New York and London: Rowman and Littlefield, 2016.

Alison LaCroix, "Rhetoric and Reality in Early American Legal History: A Response to Gordon Wood," 78 University of Chicago Law Review 733 (2011).

Max Farrand, Records of the Federal Convention, III, 94.

Alison LaCroix, "The Authority for Federalism: Madison's Negative and the Origins of Federal Ideology," 28 Law and History Review 451 (2010).

Pauline Maier, *Ratification*. New York: Simon & Schuster, 2010.

Claude Van Tyne, "Sovereignty in the American Revolution: A Historical Study," 12 Am. Hist. Rev. 529 (1907).

Charles Lofgren, "The Origins of the Tenth Amendment: History, Sovereignty, and the Problem of Constitutional Intention," in Constitutional Government in America, 331 (R. Collins ed. 1981).

Richard Morris, "We the People of the United States: The Bicentennial of a People's Revolution," 82 Am. Hist. Rev. I (1977).

Edward Corwin, "The Passing of Dual Federalism," 36 Va. L. Rev. I, 3 (1950).

Richard Posner, "Toward an Economic Theory of Federal Jurisdiction," in Symposium on Federalism, 6 Harv. J. of Law & Public Policy 41 (1982).

The Federalist Society's 2012 National Lawyers Convention, in symposium on Federalism and Federal Powers (Nov., 2012).

www.ingramcontent.com/pod-product-compliance
Lightning Source LLC
Chambersburg PA
CBHW070947200526
45161CB00001BA/11